Mastering the .NET Core Interview

Gain Expertise in MVC, ASP.NET Core, Web APIs, and EF Core, Excel in Complex Technical Interviews, Demonstrate Real-world Problem-solving Skills, and Unlock Top Career Opportunities

Nirbhay Chauhan

About the Author

Nirbhay Chauhan: Your Guide to Mastering .NET Interviews

Nirbhay Chauhan is a passionate software developer with a deep understanding of the .NET landscape. His journey began in 2000, diving headfirst into the world of computers with DOS and programming languages like C and FoxPro. This early exposure ignited a lifelong love of technology and problem-solving.

Nirbhay's career took a pivotal turn in 2009 when he achieved the coveted SCJP certification, solidifying his grasp of Java programming. But the following year, in 2010, he discovered his true calling: .NET development. This shift opened doors to exciting opportunities with various multinational corporations, both product-based and service-based.

Over the past 14 years, Nirbhay has honed his skills in a vast array of .NET technologies, including ASP.NET, C#, VB.NET, Web Forms, Win Forms, WPF, WCF, .NET Core, and SQL. His experience extends beyond coding, encompassing the successful migration of legacy applications to modern .NET frameworks. He's also played a key role in designing and architecting numerous desktop and web applications.

Nirbhay's passion extends far beyond his own expertise. He actively participates in the .NET developer community, giving and taking interviews, and even training aspiring developers eager to excel in this dynamic field. Driven by the motto "Life is teaching and I'm still learning," Nirbhay is a lifelong learner who thrives on sharing his knowledge. This zeal to connect with aspiring developers led him to create the popular YouTube channel "@DotNetInterviewCommunity," a valuable resource for anyone seeking to ace their .NET job interview.

With his extensive experience, practical knowledge, and dedication to empowering others, Nirbhay Chauhan is the ideal guide to help you navigate the .NET interview process with confidence. Let his insights in the "Mastering the .NET Core Interview" book be your key to unlocking your dream .NET career.

PREVIEW OF MY BEST SELLING BOOKS

1. Master .NET Fundamentals

2. Master C# Interview Preparation

3. .NET Developer's Interview Toolkit

4. Mastering the .NET Core Interview

5. Conquer the Azure Developer Interview

6. The Complete Front-End Interview Guide

WHY YOU SHOULD READ "MASTERING THE .NET CORE INTERVIEW"

Are you a .NET developer looking to take your career to the next level? If so, then you need to read "**Mastering the .NET Core Interview**" This comprehensive guide is your one-stop shop for mastering the essential concepts and skills required to ace your .NET interviews.

Here's why you should read this book:

- **Comprehensive Coverage:** This book covers a wide range of topics, including MVC, Asynchronous Programming, Web API & REST API, .NET Core, ASP.NET Core & EF Core.

- **Structured Approach:** The book is organized in a logical and easy-to-follow manner, making it simple to understand and retain the information.

- **Practical Advice:** Throughout the book, you'll find practical advice and tips that will help you apply the concepts you learn to real-world interview questions.

- **Time-Saving:** By reading this book, you can save yourself the time and frustration of searching for information online and trying to organize your notes.

- **Digital Detox:** This physical book is a great alternative to spending hours in front of a computer screen, allowing you to study more comfortably and efficiently.

Whether you're a beginner or an experienced .NET developer, this book is a valuable resource that will help you achieve your career goals. Don't miss out on this opportunity to level up your .NET skills and land your dream job.

Limits of Liability/Disclaimer of Warranty

The author and publisher have made their best efforts in preparing this book.

The author and publisher make no representations or warranties regarding the accuracy or completeness of the book's content.

The author and publisher specifically disclaim any implied warranties of merchantability or fitness for a particular purpose.

Warranties are limited to the descriptions contained in this paragraph and cannot be created or extended by sales representatives or written sales materials.

The accuracy, completeness, and opinions stated in the book are not guaranteed to produce particular results, and the advice and strategies may not be suitable for everyone.

The author shall be liable for any loss of profit or other commercial damages, including special, incidental, consequential, or other damages.

CONTENTS

Introduction: Your Path to .NET Interview Success XVII

1. ASP.NET MVC 1

What is ASP.NET MVC?

How ASP.NET MVC different from ASP.NET Web Forms?

What are the different types of actions in ASP.NET MVC controllers?

How does routing work in ASP.NET MVC?

How does data binding work in ASP.NET MVC?

How do you create and use Models in ASP.NET MVC?

Explain Model Binding with complex data types.

What are Model Validation techniques in ASP.NET MVC?

How to create and use Layouts for consistent UI structure?

Explain Partial Views and their benefits.

How to implement data formatting and filtering in Views?

Explain Action Filters and their usage in ASP.NET MVC.

How to create a Custom Action Filter?

What are Custom Filters and how can we create them in ASP.NET MVC?

How to handle user interactions and requests in Controllers?

Best practices for structuring and organizing Controllers.

How to implement custom routing logic?

How to implement authorization filters for access control?

How to use Dependency Injection in ASP.NET MVC?

How to integrate with external APIs using ASP.NET MVC?

How to handle errors and exceptions in Controllers?

2. Asynchronous Programming   42

What is asynchronous programming?

How does asynchronous programming differ from synchronous programming?

What is the Task class and what is its role in asynchronous
programming?

What are the async and await keywords and how do they
work?

Can we use async without await?

Example of Asynchronous Delegates.

How to handle exceptions in asynchronous methods?

How to cancel asynchronous operations?

How to use ThreadPool for asynchronous operations?

Give an example of an asynchronous callback with the help of
a delegate.

3. .NET Core History   62

.NET Core: A Journey of Evolution

A Comprehensive Look at C# Versions

4. .NET Core Fundamentals   72

What is .NET Core and how does it differ from the .NET
Framework?

Explain the key features of .NET Core.

What platforms does .NET Core support?

Describe the architecture of .NET Core.

What are the main components of the .NET Core runtime?

Explain the implicit compilation process in .NET Core.

How does .NET Core handle memory management?

What is the .NET Core CLI and how is it used?

Explain the concept of cross-platform development in .NET Core.

Explain the concept of the Base Class Library (BCL) in .NET Core.

What is the IGCToCLR interface?

What is the role of NuGet packages in .NET Core development?

What is MEF in .NET Core?

How do you deploy a .NET Core application?

How do you handle configuration in .NET Core?

What are the benefits of using SignalR in .NET Core applications, and how does it differ from traditional AJAX-based communication?

What is dependency injection and how is it implemented in .NET Core?

How does .NET Core support microservices architecture?

How does .NET Core ensure application security?

What is Kestrel and how does it fit into the ASP.NET Core architecture?

What are the differences between .Net Core and Mono?

5. ASP.NET Core   104

What is the difference between .NET Core and ASP.NET Core?

Explain the concept of middleware in ASP.NET Core.

What is dependency injection and how is it implemented in ASP.NET Core?

How do you configure services in an ASP.NET Core application?

What is the purpose of the Startup class in ASP.NET Core?

Example of startup class in ASP.NET Core.

What are the different service lifetimes in .NET Core?

How do you handle configuration in ASP.NET Core?

Explain the concept of routing in ASP.NET Core.

Explain the difference between appsettings.json and appsettings.{Environment}.json.

How do you secure an ASP.NET Core application?

Difference between app.Run and app.Use in middleware configuration.

What is a Request delegate and how is it used?

Describe the Host in ASP.NET Core.

Explain Session and State Management in ASP.NET Core.

Describe Model Binding in ASP.NET Core. Explain Custom Model Binding.

Explain Model Validation and how to perform custom validation.

What is the Options Pattern and how is it used in ASP.NET Core configuration?

How to configure and manage multiple environments in ASP.NET Core applications?

How to access the HttpContext object within an ASP.NET Core application?

What is a Change Token in ASP.NET Core Development?

Describe the URL Rewriting Middleware in ASP.NET Core and its applications.

What are the Caching or Response Caching strategies in A SP.NET Core?

Difference between In-memory and Distributed caching in ASP.NET Core.

How to enable Cross-Origin Requests (CORS) in ASP.NET Core for API access from different domains?

Describe strongly typed views and their benefits in ASP.NET Core MVC.

6. EF Core   174

What is Entity Framework Core and how does it differ from Entity Framework?

What are the different approaches to database schema generation in EF Core?

How does EF Core handle change tracking and entity state management?

Explain the role of the DbContext class in EF Core.

How LINQ is used in EF Core?

How does EF Core handle relationships between entities?

What are migrations in EF Core and how are they used to manage database schema changes?

How does EF Core support asynchronous programming?

How do you configure EF Core to use different database providers?

What are some common EF Core configuration options and their uses?

How do you handle lazy loading and eager loading of related entities in EF Core?

What are some techniques for improving EF Core query performance?

How can you optimize EF Core change tracking behavior?

What are the benefits of using raw SQL queries with EF Core?

How does EF Core handle entity inheritance?

What is shadow property mapping in EF Core?

Explain the concept of interception in EF Core.

How do you handle data seeding and initialization in EF Core?

7. WEB API & REST API   209

What is Web API?

What is REST?

How do RESTful APIs differ from traditional web services?

History of ASP.NET Web API.

How to design and develop RESTful APIs?

Explain authentication in REST API.

What are common API design patterns and best practices?

How do I get and add a JWT token via Rest API?

What is the Difference Between PUT, POST, and PATCH in RESTful API?

How to address Idempotency in REST API using C#?

Explain CRUD mapping to HTTP Verbs in REST API.

What are the various ways to manage errors in .NET Core for web APIs?

Land Your Dream .NET Job: Don't Wing Your Interview!   240

May I Ask You For A Small Favor?   241

Disclaimer   242

INTRODUCTION: YOUR PATH TO .NET INTERVIEW SUCCESS

Are you a .NET developer feeling overwhelmed by the sheer volume of information available online to prepare for interviews? Have you struggled to find a reliable source of questions and answers that truly reflect the challenges you'll face in real-world interviews?

I've been there myself. When I was preparing for my own .NET interviews, I found myself lost in a sea of blog posts, tutorials, and forums. It was incredibly difficult to determine which resources were truly valuable and which were just noise. I spent countless hours bookmarking articles and trying to organise my notes, but it was a never-ending battle.

And let's not forget the pain of trying to find that one article you read weeks ago. Revisiting information online can be a time-consuming and frustrating process.

I knew there had to be a better way. A more structured, comprehensive approach that would equip me with the knowledge and confidence to ace any .NET interview. So, I embarked on a journey to create a collection of interview questions and answers. I poured over countless resources, analysed past interview experiences, and distilled the most essential concepts into a cohesive framework.

The result is this book, "Mastering the .NET Core Interview". It's not just a collection of questions; it's a roadmap to your .NET interview success. Each chapter is designed to provide you with a deep understanding of the core concepts and technologies that are essential for .NET developers. From the software development life cycle to design patterns and database interactions, this book covers everything you need to know.

But this book offers more than just content. It's a solution to the constant struggle of finding and revisiting information online. With this book, you have all the essential knowledge at your fingertips, ready to be reviewed whenever you need it.

Additionally, in an age of digital detox, this book provides a much-needed respite from screen time. Instead of straining your eyes in front of a computer or mobile device, you can simply pick up this physical book and start studying.

By addressing these common pain points, this book offers a win-win solution for aspiring .NET developers. It provides a comprehensive resource, eliminates the frustration of searching for information online, and promotes a healthier work-life balance.

CHAPTER 1

ASP.NET MVC

What is ASP.NET MVC?

ASP.NET MVC, or ASP.NET Model-View-Controller, is a web application framework developed by Microsoft that implements the Model-View-Controller (MVC) design pattern. It offers a structured approach for building dynamic and user-friendly web applications using ASP.NET technologies.

Here's a breakdown of the key concepts:

- **Model:** Represents the data and business logic of your application. It interacts with the data store (e.g., database) and encapsulates the application's core functionality.

- **View:** Responsible for displaying the user interface (UI) based on the data provided by the model. It typically consists of HTML templates with Razor syntax for incorporating dynamic content.

- **Controller:** Acts as the intermediary between the view and the model. It handles user requests, interacts with the model to retrieve or manipulate data, and then selects the appropriate view to display the results.

Benefits of using ASP.NET MVC:

- **Separation of Concerns:** MVC promotes clean code by separating the UI, business logic, and data access layers. This improves maintainability, reusability, and testability.

- **Flexibility:** Developers have more control over the structure and functionality of their applications.

- **Improved Testability:** The clear separation of concerns allows for easier unit testing of individual components.

- **SEO Friendly:** MVC applications can be structured in a way that's search engine friendly.

How ASP.NET MVC different from ASP.NET Web Forms?

Here's a breakdown of the key differences between ASP.NET MVC and ASP.NET Web Forms:

Development Approach:

- **ASP.NET MVC:** Implements the Model-View-Controller (MVC) design pattern. Promotes separation of concerns with clear distinctions between data (model), presentation (view), and logic (controller).

- **ASP.NET Web Forms:** Employs an event-driven model. Code behind files with both UI elements and logic, leading to tighter coupling between UI and business logic.

Control Over Application Structure:

- **ASP.NET MVC:** Offers greater developer control over the application structure and URL routing. Developers can define custom routes for more flexible and SEO-friendly URLs.

- **ASP.NET Web Forms:** Uses a more file-based approach where URLs typically map to physical files (e.g., .aspx).

Testability:

- **ASP.NET MVC:** Encourages unit testing due to the separation of concerns. Individual components (models, controllers) are easier to isolate and test independently.

- **ASP.NET Web Forms:** Testing can be more challenging due to the tighter integration of UI and logic in code-behind files.

Learning Curve:

- **ASP.NET MVC:** Generally considered to have a steeper learning curve due to understanding the MVC pattern and building custom controllers and views.

- **ASP.NET Web Forms:** Often easier to learn for developers familiar with event-driven programming and traditional ASP. NET concepts.

Suitability for Projects:

- **ASP.NET MVC:** Ideal for complex, data-driven applications where flexibility, testability, and clean architecture are crucial.

- **ASP.NET Web Forms:** Suitable for simpler, event-driven applications where rapid development and easier initial learning curve are priorities.

What are the different types of actions in ASP.NET MVC controllers?

ASP.NET MVC controllers handle user requests and interactions through different types of actions. These actions are methods within the controller class that are mapped to specific HTTP verbs (GET, POST, PUT, DELETE, etc.) and URLs.

Here are the common types of actions in ASP.NET MVC controllers:

1. Index Action:

- This is the default action for a controller. It's typically invoked when a user requests the base URL for the controller (e.g., http://yourdomain/controller).

- You can define an Index action method within your controller class to handle this scenario.

2. Verb-Specific Actions:

- Actions can be decorated with attributes like HttpGet, Http-Post, HttpPut, and HttpDelete to specify the corresponding HTTP verb they handle.

- Some common examples:

  - HttpGet: Used for retrieving data, often associated with displaying information in a view.

  - HttpPost: Used for submitting data from a form, typically for creating or updating data.

  - HttpPut: Used for updating existing data resources.

  - HttpDelete: Used for deleting data resources.

3. ViewResult Action: This type of action returns a ViewResult object, which specifies the view template to be rendered for the user interface. The view template typically contains HTML and Razor syntax to display data retrieved from the model.

4. PartialViewResult Action: Similar to ViewResult, but returns a partial view, which is a reusable piece of UI that can be embedded within another view.

5. RedirectToAction Action: This action redirects the user to a different action within the same or another controller.

6. JsonResult Action: Returns data in JSON format, often used for building APIs that communicate with JavaScript or other clients.

7. ContentResult Action: Returns a plain text string as the response.

8. FileResult Action: Returns a specific file for download (e.g., PDF, image).

How does routing work in **ASP.NET MVC?**

In ASP.NET MVC, routing plays a crucial role in mapping incoming user requests to the appropriate controller action. It acts like a traffic controller, directing requests based on the URL pattern and HTTP verb.

Here's how routing works:

1. **Request Arrives:** When a user interacts with your application (e.g., clicks a link, submits a form), a web request is sent to the server. This request includes details like URL path, HTTP verb (GET, POST, etc.), and other headers.

2. **Route Matching:** The ASP.NET MVC routing engine takes over. It inspects the incoming request's URL path and compares it against registered routes.

3. **Registered Routes:** Routes are defined in your application's startup code (typically Startup.cs for ASP.NET Core or Global.asax for older ASP.NET MVC versions). They specify URL patterns and how they map to controller actions.

* **Default Route:** By default, ASP.NET MVC has a built-in route that maps requests to the following pattern: {controller}/{action}/{id}. Here, {controller} is the name of the controller class, {action} is the name of the action method within the controller, and {id} is an optional parameter.

* **Custom Routes:** You can define custom routes to handle more complex URL patterns or map different URLs to specific controllers and actions. This allows for more flexibility in URL design.

1. **Route Match Found:** If the routing engine finds a matching route for the incoming request, it extracts information like the controller name, action name, and any parameters included in the URL.

2. **Controller Action Execution:** Based on the matched route, the routing engine then invokes the corresponding controller action method. This action method handles the request logic and interacts with the model to retrieve or manipulate data.

3. **Response Generation:** The controller action performs the necessary operations and then typically returns a result (e.g., a view, data in JSON format, etc.). This result is then sent back to the user's browser as a response.

How does data binding work in ASP.NET MVC?

Data binding in ASP.NET MVC plays a vital role in bridging the gap between user input (from forms or requests) and your application's model objects. It automatically converts data from the request into usable objects within your controllers and views.

Here's a breakdown of how data binding works:

1. User Interaction:

- Users interact with your web application through forms, providing input in text boxes, dropdowns, or other UI elements.

2. Form Submission:

- When a user submits a form, the browser sends an HTTP request (typically a POST request) to the server. This request includes the form data as key-value pairs (e.g., name="John", email="[email address removed]").

3. Model Binding Process:

- ASP.NET MVC receives the request and triggers the model binding process.

- The model binder inspects the request data and attempts to map it to a corresponding model object in your application.

Key Aspects of Model Binding:

- **Model Binder Selection:** ASP.NET MVC uses a default model binder for simple data types (e.g., strings, integers). For complex types (custom classes), it searches for a custom model binder or relies on reflection to map properties.

- **Property Matching:** The model binder tries to match the form field names (keys) with the properties of the model object. Case-insensitive matching is usually performed.

- **Type Conversion:** If necessary, the model binder attempts to convert the data from the request into the corresponding data type of the model property (e.g., string to integer).

4. Populating the Model:

- If the model binding is successful, the model binder populates the properties of the model object with the converted data from the request.

5. Utilizing Data in Controllers and Views:

- The controller can then access the populated model object through the action method's parameters. This data can be used for various purposes, such as:

  - Validating user input

  - Performing business logic operations

  - Passing data to the view for display

How do you create and use Models in ASP.NET MVC?

Models are the heart of an ASP.NET MVC application. They represent the data and business logic of your application and play a crucial role in managing and manipulating information. Here's how to create and use models effectively:

1. Model Creation:

- Models are typically defined as plain old CLR objects (POCO) classes in C#.

- These classes contain properties that represent the data your application needs to work with.

- For example, a Product model might have properties like Id, Name, Price, and Description.

2. Data Annotations (Optional):

- ASP.NET MVC offers data annotations, which are attributes you can apply to model properties.

- These annotations provide information about the data, such as:

  - **Validation rules:** Specify requirements for data types, lengths, or custom validation logic.

  - **Display information:** Define how properties are displayed in views (e.g., labels, formatting).

3. Example Model with Data Annotations:

Code snippet

```
public class Product

{

public int Id { get; set; }

[Required]

[StringLength(50)]

public string Name { get; set; }

[DataType(DataType.Currency)]

public decimal Price { get; set; }

[MaxLength(200)]

public string Description { get; set; }

}
```

In this example:

- Required attribute ensures the Name property is filled.

- StringLength limits the name length to 50 characters.

- DataType displays the Price with currency formatting.

- MaxLength sets a maximum length for the Description.

4. Model Usage in Controllers:

- Controllers can accept models as parameters in their action methods.

- These model objects are typically populated through data binding during user interactions (e.g., form submissions).

- The controller can then access the data in the model properties and perform operations like:

  - Validating user input (using data annotations or custom logic)

  - Retrieving data from a database (using Entity Framework or other data access methods)

  - Updating data in the database

5. Model Usage in Views:

- Views typically display data from the model.

- ASP.NET MVC offers Razor syntax, which allows you to embed expressions within HTML code.

- You can use these expressions to access model properties and display data dynamically.

Example View with Razor Syntax:

<h1>Product Details</h1>

<ul>

<li>Name: @Model.Name</li>

<li>Price: @Model.Price</li>

<li>Description: @Model.Description</li>

</ul>

In this example:

- @Model refers to the model object passed to the view.

- Razor syntax allows you to access model properties directly.

Explain Model Binding with complex data types.

ASP.NET MVC's model binding automatically maps incoming form data to properties of your model objects. While simple types like strings, integers, and booleans are straightforward, handling complex data types requires a deeper understanding.

How it works:

- **Prefix-based matching:** The model binder uses a prefix-based matching system to identify properties within complex types. For instance, if you have a Customer model with a Address property, the form fields would be named Customer.Address.Street, Customer.Address.City, etc.

- **Recursive binding:** The model binder recursively binds properties of complex types, creating nested objects as needed.

- **Custom model binders:** For complex scenarios, you can create custom model binders to handle specific binding logic.

Example:

public class Customer

{

public int Id { get; set; }

public string Name { get; set; }

public Address Address { get; set; }

}

public class Address

{

public string Street { get; set; }

```
public string City { get; set; }

public string ZipCode { get; set; }

}
```

In your view, you'd have form elements like:

```
<input type="text" name="Name" />

<input type="text" name="Address.Street" />

<input type="text" name="Address.City" />

<input type="text" name="Address.ZipCode" />
```

When the form is submitted, the model binder automatically creates a Customer object and populates its properties based on the form data, including the nested Address object.

Key points to remember:

- **Naming conventions:** Ensure form field names match the property names in your model for successful binding.

- **Model validation:** Use data annotations to validate complex type properties.

- **Custom model binders:** For complex scenarios, create custom model binders to handle specific binding logic.

What are Model Validation techniques in ASP.NET MVC?

In ASP.NET MVC, ensuring data integrity is crucial. Model validation techniques help you enforce rules and ensure the data submitted by users or retrieved from external sources meets your application's requirements. Here's an overview of common validation techniques:

1. Data Annotations:

- Built-in attributes applied directly to model properties.

- Offer a convenient and declarative way to define validation rules.

- Some common data annotation attributes:

  - Required: Ensures a property has a value.

  - StringLength: Limits the length of a string property.

  - Range: Defines a valid range for numerical properties.

  - RegularExpression: Validates data against a specific pattern.

  - EmailAddress: Ensures a valid email address format.

Example:

public class User

{

[Required]

public string Name { get; set; }

[EmailAddress]

public string Email { get; set; }

[Range(18, 120)]

public int Age { get; set; }

}

2. Custom Validation Attributes:

- Extend existing data annotation attributes or create entirely new ones to handle specific validation logic.

- Useful for complex validation scenarios beyond built-in options.

3. Fluent Validation Libraries:

- Third-party libraries like FluentValidation offer a more robust and flexible approach to validation.

- Define validation rules in a fluent manner, providing clearer and more readable code.

- Often provide features like cascading validation or automatic validation message generation.

4. Model Validation Results:

- Once validation is performed, the model binding process captures validation errors in a ModelStateDictionary object.

- Controllers can access this dictionary to check for errors and display appropriate messages to the user.

5. Model State Validation Helpers in Views:

- ASP.NET MVC offers Razor syntax helpers like @Html.ValidationMessage and @Html.ValidationSummary to display validation errors directly within views.

- These helpers simplify displaying error messages in a user-friendly format.

How to create and use Layouts for consistent UI structure?

Layouts in ASP.NET MVC provide a consistent structure and appearance across multiple views. They encapsulate the common elements of your application, such as header, footer, navigation, and content placeholders.

Creating a Layout

1. **Create a new view:** Right-click on the Shared folder in your Views folder and add a new view. Name it _Layout.cshtml (or any desired name).

2. **Design the layout:** Within the _Layout.cshtml file, define the HTML structure for your layout. Include placeholders for dy-

namic content using the @RenderBody() helper.

3. **Define content placeholders:** Use the @RenderBody() helper to specify where the content of individual views will be inserted.

Example Layout (_Layout.cshtml)

Razor CSHTML

```
<!DOCTYPE html>

<html>

<head>

<title>My Application</title>

</head>

<body>

<header>

</header>

<nav>

</nav>

<div class="container">

@RenderBody()

</div>

<footer>

</footer>

</body>

</html>
```

Using Layouts in Views

1. **Set the layout:** In your view, use the @{ Layout = "~/Views /Shared/_Layout.cshtml"; } directive at the top of the view to specify the layout to use.

2. **Add content:** Place your view-specific content within the body of the view.

Example View:

Razor CSHTML

```
@{

Layout = "~/Views/Shared/_Layout.cshtml";

}

<h2>Home Page</h2>

<p>This is the content for the home page.</p>
```

Explain Partial Views and their benefits.

Partial Views are reusable chunks of view logic that can be rendered within another view. They are similar to user controls in Web Forms but are specifically designed for MVC.

Benefits of Partial Views:

- **Reusability:** A partial view can be reused across multiple main views, reducing code duplication.

- **Maintainability:** Changes made to a partial view are reflected in all pages using it.

- **Modularization:** Helps break down complex views into smaller, manageable components.

- **Performance:** Can improve performance by reducing the amount of HTML sent to the client.

Creating a Partial View:

- Create a new .cshtml file within the Shared folder of your Views directory.

- Design the content for the partial view.

Rendering a Partial View:

You can render a partial view using the Html.Partial or Html.RenderP artial methods within your main view.

- **Html.Partial:** Returns a string containing the rendered HTML of the partial view.

- **Html.RenderPartial:** Directly writes the rendered HTML to the output stream.

Example:

Razor CSHTML

// In your main view

@{

var products = new List<Product> { ... };

}

<ul>

@foreach (var product in products)

{

<li>@product.Name - @product.Price</li>

}

</ul>

@Html.Partial("_ProductDetails", new { Product = products.First() })

Razor CSHTML

// In your partial view (_ProductDetails.cshtml)

<h2>Product Details</h2>

<p>Name: @Model.Name</p>

<p>Price: @Model.Price</p>

<p>Description: @Model.Description</p>

How to implement data formatting and filtering in Views?

ASP.NET MVC provides several mechanisms to format and filter data within your views, enhancing the presentation and usability of your application.

Data Formatting

1. Built-in Formatters:

- Leverage built-in formatters for common data types like dates, numbers, and currencies.

- Use @String.Format or String.Format for custom formatting.

Example:

Razor CSHTML

@Model.Price.ToString("C") // Format as currency

@String.Format("{0:dd/MM/yyyy}", Model.OrderDate) // Custom date format

2. Display Templates:

- Create reusable templates for complex data types.

- Define how objects should be rendered in views.

3. Custom Display Templates:

- Create custom display templates for specific data types or scenarios.

- Override default rendering behavior.

4. Editor Templates:

- Similar to display templates, but used for editing data.

- Often used in forms for complex object editing.

Data Filtering

1. LINQ:

- Use LINQ (Language Integrated Query) to filter data within your controller before passing it to the view.

- This approach is efficient for complex filtering logic.

Example:

var filteredProducts = products.Where(p => p.Price > 100);

return View(filteredProducts);

2. Filtering in Views:

- While less common, you can perform basic filtering within the view using Razor syntax, but it's generally less efficient for complex scenarios.

3. Client-Side Filtering:

- For interactive filtering experiences, use JavaScript libraries like jQuery or DataTables.

- These libraries allow users to filter data dynamically without full page reloads.

Explain Action Filters and their usage in ASP.NET MVC.

Action filters in ASP.NET MVC are powerful tools that allow you to intercept the execution pipeline of an action method in your controllers. They provide a way to inject common functionality or logic before, after, or around the actual execution of the action method. This functionality can range from handling authorization and logging to manipulating data or performing cleanup tasks.

Here's a breakdown of Action Filters:

Types of Action Filters:

- **Authorization Filters:** These filters are responsible for checking user permissions and authorization to access specific actions. They implement the IAuthorizationFilter interface and can be used to restrict access based on roles, claims, or custom logic.

    - Example: [Authorize(Roles = "Admin")] attribute restricts access to the action for users with the "Admin" role.

- **Action Filters:** These filters provide more general pre- and post-action execution behavior. They implement the IActionFilter interface and offer methods like OnActionExecuting and OnActionExecuted to perform logic before and after the action method, respectively.

    - Example: A custom action filter that logs all incoming requests before the action executes.

- **Result Filters:** These filters intercept the result returned by an action method. They implement the IResultFilter interface and offer methods like OnResultExecuting and OnResultExecuted to modify the result object or perform additional processing before the final response is sent back to the client.

    - Example: A custom result filter that compresses the response content for bandwidth optimization.

- **Exception Filters:** These filters handle exceptions that occur during action execution. They implement the IExceptionFilter interface and provide a way to handle exceptions gracefully, log them, or redirect users to error pages.

    - Example: A custom exception filter that logs all unhandled exceptions and redirects the user to a generic error page.

Applying Action Filters:

- **Attributes:** You can apply action filters to individual actions or entire controllers using attributes. These attributes represent specific filter implementations.

- **Global Filters:** You can register filters globally in the Application_Start method of your application to apply them to all controllers or specific actions across your application.

How to create a Custom Action Filter?

Below are the steps required for creating a Custom Action Filter in ASP.NET MVC:

Understanding the Basics:

- **IActionFilter:** Defines methods to execute code before and after an action method.

- **ActionFilterAttribute:** Base class for custom action filters.

Steps to create a custom action filter:

1. **Create a new class:** Inherit from ActionFilterAttribute and implement IActionFilter.

2. **Override methods:** Override OnActionExecuting and OnActionExecuted methods to implement your custom logic.

3. **Apply the filter:** Use the custom filter attribute on controllers or action methods.

Example:

```
using System;

using System.Web.Mvc;

public class LoggingFilter : ActionFilterAttribute, IActionFilter
{
```

```csharp
public override void OnActionExecuting(ActionExecutingContext filterContext)

{

// Code to execute before the action method

// e.g., log request information, check authorization, etc.

base.OnActionExecuting(filterContext);

}

public override void OnActionExecuted(ActionExecutedContext filterContext)

{

// Code to execute after the action method

// e.g., log response, handle exceptions, etc.

base.OnActionExecuted(filterContext);

}

}
```

Applying the Filter:

At Controller Level:[LoggingFilter]

```csharp
public class HomeController : Controller

{

// ...

}
```

At Action Level:public class HomeController : Controller

```csharp
{

[LoggingFilter]
```

```
public ActionResult Index()

{

// ...

}

}
```

Additional Considerations:

- **Global Filters:** Register custom filters globally in Global.asax for application-wide application.

- **Filter Order:** Multiple filters can be applied to a controller or action. The execution order is determined by the order in which they are registered.

- **Context Information:** The filterContext parameter provides access to information about the current request, controller, action, and result.

- **Performance:** Be mindful of performance implications when using custom filters, especially for computationally intensive tasks.

What are Custom Filters and how can we create them in ASP.NET MVC?

Custom filters in ASP.NET MVC extend the built-in filter functionality by allowing you to define your own logic to intercept and modify the request processing pipeline. They offer a powerful way to centralize common tasks and functionalities across your application.

Here's a breakdown of creating custom filters:

Understanding Filter Interfaces: ASP.NET MVC provides various filter interfaces for different aspects of the request pipeline:

- **IActionFilter:** Intercepts action execution before and after the action method is called.

- **IAuthorizationFilter:** Performs authorization checks before the action method is called.

- **IResultFilter:** Intercepts the result returned by the action method before it's sent back to the client.

- **IExceptionFilter:** Handles exceptions that occur during action execution.

Steps to Create a Custom Filter:

1. **Choose the Interface:** Select the appropriate filter interface based on your desired functionality (e.g., IActionFilter for pre- and post-action logic).

2. **Create a Class:** Inherit from the chosen interface and define its methods.

3. **Implement Methods:** Override the interface methods to implement your custom logic:

   - OnActionExecuting (IActionFilter): Code to execute before the action method.

   - OnActionExecuted (IActionFilter): Code to execute after the action method.

   - OnAuthorization (IAuthorizationFilter): Perform authorization checks.

   - OnResultExecuting (IResultFilter): Modify the result before sending to the client.

   - OnResultExecuted (IResultFilter): Perform additional processing after result generation.

   - OnException (IExceptionFilter): Handle exceptions.

4. **Apply the Filter:** Use a custom filter attribute derived from FilterAttribute to apply the filter to controllers or actions.

For creating Custom Filter we can take the help of the above question example.

How to handle user interactions and requests in Controllers?

Controllers are the heart of ASP.NET MVC applications, responsible for handling user requests, processing data, and returning appropriate responses. Here's how controllers work:

1. Routing:

- When a user requests a URL, the ASP.NET MVC routing engine matches it to a registered route.

- This route determines which controller and action method should handle the request.

2. Controller Action:

- The matched controller action is invoked.

- This action method typically contains the business logic for processing the request.

- You can define various types of actions:

  - **HttpGet:** Handles GET requests (e.g., displaying data).

  - **HttpPost:** Handles POST requests (e.g., submitting forms).

  - **HttpPut:** Handles PUT requests (e.g., updating data).

  - **HttpDelete:** Handles DELETE requests (e.g., deleting data).

3. Data Binding:

- ASP.NET MVC automatically binds form data to model objects.

- This simplifies data handling within controller actions.

4. Processing Logic: The controller action can perform various operations:

- Retrieve data from databases or other sources.

- Validate user input.

- Perform business logic.

- Update data.

- Redirect to other actions or views.

5. Returning Results: Controller actions typically return a result. Common result types include:

- **ViewResult:** Renders a specified view with data.

- **JsonResult:** Returns data in JSON format.

- **RedirectResult:** Redirects the user to a different URL.

- **ContentResult:** Returns a plain text string.

Example:

```
public class HomeController : Controller

{

public IActionResult Index()

{

// Retrieve data from a database or other source

var products = _productRepository.GetAll();

// Pass the data to the view

return View(products);

}
```

```
[HttpPost]

public IActionResult Create(Product product)

{

// Validate the product data

if (ModelState.IsValid)

{

// Save the product to the database

_productRepository.Add(product);

return RedirectToAction("Index");

}

// If validation fails, redisplay the view with error messages

return View(product);

}

}
```

Best practices for structuring and organizing Controllers.

Effective controller organization is crucial for creating maintainable and scalable ASP.NET MVC applications. Here are some best practices to follow:

1. Use a Consistent Naming Convention:

- Adhere to a consistent naming convention for controllers and action methods (e.g., PascalCase).

- Use meaningful names that reflect their purpose.

2. Group Related Actions:

- Organize controllers into logical groups based on functionality.

- This makes it easier to find and manage related actions.

3. Avoid Overloading Controllers:

- Keep controllers focused on specific areas of functionality.

- Avoid creating overly large controllers with many actions.

- Consider breaking down large controllers into smaller, more specialized ones.

4. Utilize Action Filters:

- Use action filters to implement cross-cutting concerns like authorization, logging, and caching.

- This helps keep your controllers clean and focused on core business logic.

5. Consider Dependency Injection:

- Inject dependencies into controllers using dependency injection to improve testability and maintainability.

- This allows you to decouple controllers from concrete implementations of services.

6. Use View Models:

- Create view models to represent data that needs to be passed to views.

- This helps separate the presentation layer from the business logic.

7. Follow RESTful Principles:

- If applicable, design your controllers to adhere to RESTful principles for a more structured and maintainable API.

- Use appropriate HTTP verbs (GET, POST, PUT, DELETE)

for CRUD operations.

8. Leverage Conventions:

- ASP.NET MVC uses conventions to simplify development.

- Follow these conventions whenever possible to reduce boiler-plate code.

9. Consider Using Areas:

- For larger applications, use areas to organize controllers and views into logical modules.

- This can help manage complexity and improve code organization.

10. Write Unit Tests:

- Write unit tests for your controllers to ensure their correctness and prevent regressions.

- Test-driven development (TDD) can be a valuable approach to writing well-structured controllers.

How to implement custom routing logic?

Custom routing in ASP.NET MVC allows you to define your own URL patterns and map them to specific controllers and actions, providing more flexibility and control over how your application handles requests.

1. Register Custom Routes:

- In your Startup.cs file (or Global.asax in older ASP.NET MVC versions), register custom routes using the MapRoute method of the RouteCollection class.

- This method takes a route name, URL pattern, and defaults dictionary as parameters.

Example:

```
public void ConfigureRoutes(IRouteBuilder routes)

{

routes.MapRoute(

name: "CustomRoute",

url: "blog/{year}/{month}/{day}/{title}",

defaults: new { controller = "Blog", action = "Details" }

);

}
```

2. Define URL Patterns:

- The url parameter in MapRoute defines the URL pattern to match incoming requests.

- Use {controller}, {action}, and {id} placeholders to represent dynamic segments of the URL.

3. Specify Defaults:

- The defaults dictionary defines default values for controller, action, and other parameters.

- If a segment of the URL is not specified in the request, the default values are used.

4. Handle Custom Routes in Controllers:

- Create controller actions that correspond to the defined URL patterns.

- Use route data to extract parameters from the URL and process the request accordingly.

Example:

```
public class BlogController : Controller
```

```
{

public IActionResult Details(int year, int month, int day, string title)

{

// Retrieve blog post based on the parameters

var blogPost = _blogRepository.GetBlogPost(year, month, day, title);

if (blogPost != null)

{

return View(blogPost);

}

return NotFound();

}

}
```

Key Points:

- **Route Priority:** Custom routes are evaluated in the order they are registered. The first matching route is used.

- **Constraints:** You can apply constraints to URL segments to enforce specific validation rules (e.g., numeric, regular expression).

- **Optional Parameters:** Use the ? character to make URL segments optional.

- **Route Data:** Access route data within your controller actions using the RouteData property.

Benefits of Custom Routing:

- **SEO-Friendly URLs:** Create more readable and search engine-friendly URLs.

- **Flexibility:** Customize URL structures to match your application's requirements.

- **Dynamic Routing:** Handle dynamic URL segments for features like pagination or filtering.

How to implement authorization filters for access control?

Authorization filters in ASP.NET MVC provide a mechanism to control access to specific actions or controllers based on user permissions or roles. They are essential for securing your application and preventing unauthorized access to sensitive resources.

1. Create a Custom Authorization Filter: Inherit from AuthorizationFilterAttribute and implement the OnAuthorization method.

public class AuthorizeAdminAttribute : AuthorizeAttribute

{

public override void OnAuthorization(AuthorizationContext filterContext)

{

if (!filterContext.HttpContext.User.IsInRole("Admin"))

{

// Acccss dcnicd

filterContext.Result = new RedirectToActionResult("AccessDenied", "Home", null);

}

}

}

2. Apply the Filter: Use the custom attribute on controllers or action methods to apply the authorization filter.

```
[AuthorizeAdmin]
```

```
public class AdminController : Controller
```

```
{
```

```
// ...
```

```
}
```

3. Customize Authorization Logic:

- Implement your desired authorization logic within the OnAuthorization method.

- Check user roles, claims, or any other criteria to determine if access is granted.

- If access is denied, set the Result property of Authorization-Context to redirect to a login page, error page, or handle the denial in another way.

4. Custom Authorization Filters:

- Create custom authorization filters for more complex scenarios.

- You can implement custom logic, combine multiple authorization requirements, or integrate with external authentication providers.

Example: Role-Based Authorization

```
public class AuthorizeRolesAttribute : AuthorizeAttribute
```

```
{
```

```
private readonly string[] _allowedRoles;
```

```
public AuthorizeRolesAttribute(params string[] roles)
```

```
{
```

```
_allowedRoles = roles;
```

```
}

public override void OnAuthorization(AuthorizationContext filter-
Context)

{

var user = filterContext.HttpContext.User;

if (!user.Identity.IsAuthenticated || !user.IsInAnyRole(_allowedRoles))

{

// Access denied

filterContext.Result = new RedirectToActionResult("AccessDenied",
"Home", null);

}

}

}
```

Key Considerations:

- **Roles and Permissions:** Define roles and assign permissions to them.

- **User Claims:** Use claims-based authorization for more granular control.

- **Custom Logic:** Implement custom authorization logic based on your application's requirements.

- **Error Handling:** Provide appropriate feedback to users when authorization fails.

How to use Dependency Injection in ASP.NET MVC?

Dependency injection (DI) is a powerful design pattern that promotes loose coupling and improves testability in ASP.NET MVC applications. Here's how you can use it effectively:

1. Dependency Injection Basics:

- **Principle:** Objects don't create their own dependencies (other objects they rely on).

- **Benefits:**

  - Easier to test components in isolation.

  - More flexible application structure.

  - Improved maintainability.

2. Implementing DI: There are two main approaches to dependency injection in ASP.NET MVC:

A. Using Built-in ASP.NET Core DI:

- ASP.NET Core offers built-in DI features through the IServiceCollection interface.

- Register your services (interfaces and implementations) in the ConfigureServices method of your Startup.cs file.

public void ConfigureServices(IServiceCollection services)

{

services.AddControllersWithViews();

services.AddTransient<IProductService, ProductService>(); // Register service and implementation

}

- Inject dependencies into your controllers using constructor injection:

public class HomeController : Controller

{

private readonly IProductService _productService;

```
public HomeController(IProductService productService)

{

_productService = productService;

}

public IActionResult Index()

{

var products = _productService.GetAllProducts();

// ...

}

}
```

B. Using Third-Party DI Containers:

- Popular choices include Autofac, Ninject, and StructureMap.

- These provide additional features and configuration options compared to built-in DI.

- Follow the specific documentation of your chosen container for setup and usage.

3. Common Scenarios for DI:

- Injecting repositories for data access.

- Injecting logging services.

- Injecting configuration settings.

- Injecting mailers or other communication services.

4. Key Considerations:

- **Interface vs. Concrete Class:** Inject dependencies as interfaces, not concrete implementations, for flexibility.

- **Lifetime Scopes:** Choose the appropriate lifetime scope for your service (Transient, Scoped, Singleton) depending on its usage pattern.

- **Testability:** DI allows injecting mock objects for unit testing, making your controllers easier to test in isolation.

How to integrate with external APIs using ASP.NET MVC?

Integrating with external APIs in ASP.NET MVC applications unlocks a wide range of functionalities and data sources. Here's a breakdown of the key steps:

1. Choose an API and Understand its Documentation:

- Identify the external API you want to connect with and thoroughly review its documentation.

- Familiarize yourself with its endpoints, authentication methods, request and response formats (e.g., JSON, XML).

2. Install a Client Library (Optional):

- Some APIs offer official client libraries for specific programming languages like C#.

- These libraries simplify communication by providing pre-built classes and methods for interacting with the API.

3. Making HTTP Requests:

- Use System.Net.Http namespace classes like HttpClient to make HTTP requests to the API endpoints.

- Set headers, parameters, and the request body (if applicable) based on the API's requirements.

4. Handling Responses:

- Read the response content using HttpClient.GetStringAsync or deserialize JSON responses using libraries like Newtonsoft

.Json.

- Check the response status code for success (200 OK) or errors. Handle potential exceptions or error codes gracefully.

5. Authentication Considerations:

- Some APIs require authentication tokens, API keys, or other credentials.

- Include the required authentication details in the request headers or body according to the API's specifications.

Example: Using HttpClient to call a Weather API:

```
public class WeatherService

{

private readonly HttpClient _httpClient;

public WeatherService(HttpClient httpClient)

{

_httpClient = httpClient;

}

public async Task<WeatherData> GetCurrentWeather(string city)

{

var apiKey = "YOUR_API_KEY"; // Replace with your actual API key

var url = $"https://<apiurl>?q={city}&apikey={apiKey}";

var response = await _httpClient.GetAsync(url);

if (response.IsSuccessStatusCode)

{

var responseString = await response.Content.ReadAsStringAsync();
```

var weatherData = JsonConvert.DeserializeObject<WeatherData>(res
ponseString);

return weatherData;

}

// Handle errors

throw new Exception("Error retrieving weather data");

}

}

Additional Considerations:

- **Asynchronous Programming:** Use asynchronous methods like HttpClient.GetAsync to improve performance and avoid blocking threads.

- **Error Handling:** Implement robust error handling to catch exceptions and handle API failures gracefully.

- **Caching (Optional):** Consider caching API responses to reduce redundant calls and improve performance.

- **Security:** Pay close attention to security when working with external APIs, especially when handling sensitive data.

How to handle errors and exceptions in Controllers?

Proper error handling is crucial for creating robust and user-friendly ASP.NET MVC applications. Here are some best practices:

1. Use Exception Filters:

- Implement IExceptionFilter to capture and handle exceptions globally.

- This allows you to centralize error handling logic and provide a consistent response.

Example:

```
public class GlobalExceptionHandler : IExceptionFilter

{

public void OnException(ExceptionContext filterContext)

{

// Log the exception

Logger.LogError(filterContext.Exception);

// Redirect to an error page or return a custom error response

filterContext.Result = new RedirectToActionResult("Error", "Home",
null);

}

}
```

2. Specific Exception Handling:

- For specific exceptions, handle them within your controller actions using try-catch blocks.

- Provide informative error messages to the user.

Example:

```
public IActionResult Create(Product product)

{

try

{

_productRepository.Add(product);

return RedirectToAction("Index");

}
```

```
catch (Exception ex)

{

// Log the exception

Logger.LogError(ex);

// Return a view with an error message

ModelState.AddModelError("", "An error occurred while creating the product.");

return View(product);

}

}
```

3. Custom Error Pages:

- Create custom error pages to provide informative and user-friendly messages.

- Use the HandleErrorAttribute to automatically redirect to a custom error page.

4. Logging:

- Implement logging to record errors and track application behavior.

- Use logging frameworks like NLog, Serilog, or Microsoft's built-in logging to log exceptions and other relevant information.

5. User-Friendly Error Messages:

- Avoid displaying generic error messages that might reveal sensitive information.

- Provide clear and informative messages that guide the user on how to resolve the issue.

6. Test Error Handling:

- Write unit tests to verify that your error handling mechanisms work as expected.

- Simulate various error scenarios to ensure your application responds gracefully.

Additional Tips:

- Consider using a global error handler in Global.asax for application-wide exception handling.

- Use HTTP status codes (e.g., 404, 500) to indicate different types of errors.

- Provide a way for users to report errors or contact support.

CHAPTER 2

ASYNCHRONOUS PROGRAMMING

What is asynchronous programming?

Asynchronous programming is a programming paradigm that allows tasks to be executed independently of the main application thread, improving responsiveness and preventing the application from freezing. In contrast to synchronous programming, where tasks are executed sequentially, asynchronous tasks can run concurrently, allowing the application to continue processing other tasks while waiting for the asynchronous task to complete.

Key benefits of asynchronous programming:

- **Improved Responsiveness:** Asynchronous tasks can run in the background, preventing the main thread from being blocked and ensuring that the application remains responsive to user input.

- **Scalability:** Asynchronous programming can help to improve the scalability of applications by allowing them to handle more concurrent requests.

- **Efficient Resource Utilization:** Asynchronous tasks can be executed on separate threads, allowing for more efficient use of system resources.

Common use cases for asynchronous programming:

- **Long-running tasks:** Tasks that take a significant amount of time to complete, such as I/O operations, database queries, or network requests.

- **Parallel processing:** Tasks that can be executed concurrently to improve performance.

- **User interface responsiveness:** Ensuring that applications remain responsive to user input while performing background tasks.

In .NET, asynchronous programming is typically implemented using the async and await keywords, which provide a simplified syntax for writing asynchronous code.

How does asynchronous programming differ from synchronous programming?

Synchronous Programming

- Tasks are executed sequentially, one after the other.

- The main thread is blocked while waiting for a task to complete.

- Can lead to unresponsive user interfaces if tasks are long-running.

Asynchronous Programming

- Tasks are executed independently of the main thread, allowing other tasks to continue while the asynchronous task is running.

- The main thread is not blocked while waiting for the asynchronous task to complete.

- Improves application responsiveness and prevents freezing.

Key Differences:

Example: Synchronous:

```
var result = DoLongRunningTask();
```

Console.WriteLine(result);

Asynchronous:

var task = Task.Run(() => DoLongRunningTask());

var result = await task;

Console.WriteLine(result);

In the synchronous example, the main thread is blocked until DoLongRunningTask is completed. In the asynchronous example, the main thread can continue with other tasks while DoLongRunningTask is running.

What is the Task class and what is its role in asynchronous programming?

The Task class in .NET is a fundamental building block for asynchronous programming. It represents an asynchronous operation that can be created, started, awaited, and managed.

Key Roles of the Task Class:

- **Represents Asynchronous Operations:** A Task object encapsulates an asynchronous operation, allowing you to manage its state, results, and exceptions.

- **Task Creation:** You can create Task objects using various methods, such as Task.Run, Task.Factory.StartNew, or by creating a custom Task subclass.

- **Task Execution:** Once created, a Task can be started by calling its Start method. This will begin executing the asynchronous operation on a background thread.

- **Task Waiting:** You can use the await keyword to pause the execution of an asynchronous method until a Task completes. This ensures that the main thread is not blocked while waiting for the asynchronous operation to finish.

- **Task Results:** If the asynchronous operation produces a result, you can access it using the Result property of the Task object.

- **Task Exceptions:** If an exception occurs during the asynchronous operation, it can be accessed using the Exception property of the Task object.

- **Task Cancellation:** You can use a CancellationToken to cancel a Task if necessary.

Example:

```
async Task<int> CalculateFactorialAsync(int n)

{

await Task.Delay(1000); // Simulate a long-running task

int result = 1;

for (int i = 1; i <= n; i++)

{

result *= i;

}

return result;

}

async Task Main()

{

var task = CalculateFactorialAsync(5);

int factorial = await task;

Console.WriteLine($"Factorial of 5: {factorial}");

}
```

What are the async and await keywords and how do they work?

The async and await keywords in C# are used to simplify asynchronous programming, making it easier to write code that can perform long-running tasks without blocking the main thread.

async Keyword:

- Indicates that a method is asynchronous and can be awaited.

- Marks the method as potentially using asynchronous operations.

- Allows the use of the await keyword within the method.

await Keyword:

- Pauses the execution of the current method until the result of an asynchronous operation is available.

- Returns the result of the asynchronous operation when it's complete.

- Can only be used within an async method.

How they work together:

1. **async Method:** When an async method is called, it starts executing on the current thread.

2. **await Expression:** When the await keyword is encountered, the method's execution is paused, and the control is returned to the caller.

3. **Task Completion:** The asynchronous operation continues to execute on a background thread.

4. **Result Retrieval:** When the asynchronous operation completes, the await expression resumes execution and returns the result of the operation.

Example:

```
async Task<int> GetNumberAsync()

{

await Task.Delay(1000); // Simulate an asynchronous operation

return 42;

}

async Task Main()

{

int result = await GetNumberAsync();

Console.WriteLine(result);

}
```

In this example, the GetNumberAsync method is marked as async. The await keyword is used to pause the execution of the Main method until the GetNumberAsync task completes. When the task completes, the await expression returns the result (42), and the Main method continues execution.

Key Points:

- async and await are used together to write asynchronous code in a more readable and maintainable way.

- await can only be used within an async method.

- The async keyword does not guarantee that the method will be executed asynchronously.

- The await keyword pauses the execution of the current method until the asynchronous operation completes.

Can we use async without await?

Yes, you can use the async keyword without the await keyword in C#.

However, doing so is generally not recommended as it can lead to unexpected behavior and performance issues.

Here's why:

- **No Asynchronous Execution:** When you use async without await, the method is still marked as asynchronous, but it doesn't actually execute asynchronously. It's essentially a regular synchronous method.

- **Potential Deadlocks:** If you use async without await and call another asynchronous method within it, you can introduce deadlocks. This happens because the calling method and the called method might both be waiting for each other to complete, resulting in a deadlock.

- **Reduced Readability:** Using async without await can make your code harder to understand, as it might not be clear that the method is intended to be asynchronous.

When might you use async without await?

- **Creating Asynchronous Delegates:** You can use async to create asynchronous delegates, which can be used to pass asynchronous methods as arguments to other methods.

- **Custom Asynchronous Patterns:** In some advanced scenarios, you might need to use async without await to implement custom asynchronous patterns.

Example of Asynchronous Delegates.

```csharp
public delegate Task<int> AsyncOperation();

async Task Main()
```

```
{

// Create an asynchronous delegate

AsyncOperation calculateFactorial = async () =>

{

await Task.Delay(1000); // Simulate a long-running task

return 5!;

};

// Pass the delegate to another method

int result = await PerformAsyncOperation(calculateFactorial);

Console.WriteLine($"Factorial of 5: {result}");

}

async Task<int> PerformAsyncOperation(AsyncOperation operation)

{

return await operation();

}
```

In this example:

1. **AsyncOperation delegate:** This delegate defines a method
   that returns a Task<int>, representing an asynchronous operation.

2. **Lambda expression:** The lambda expression assigned to calculateFactorial represents an asynchronous operation that cal-
   culates the factorial of 5.

3. **Passing the delegate:** The calculateFactorial delegate is passed
   as an argument to the PerformAsyncOperation method.

4. **Invoking the delegate:** The PerformAsyncOperation method
   invokes the delegate using the await keyword, allowing for

asynchronous execution.

How to handle exceptions in asynchronous methods?

When working with asynchronous methods in C#, it's essential to handle exceptions appropriately to ensure the reliability and robustness of your applications. Here are some key strategies:

1. Use try-catch Blocks: Enclose asynchronous methods within try-catch blocks to catch exceptions that might occur during the asynchronous operation. Handle exceptions gracefully and provide informative error messages to the user.

Example:

```csharp
async Task<int> CalculateFactorialAsync(int n)

{

try

{

await Task.Delay(1000); // Simulate a long-running task

if (n < 0)

{

throw new ArgumentException("n must be non-negative.");

}

int result = 1;

for (int i = 1; i <= n; i++)

{

result *= i;

}

return result;
```

```
}

catch (ArgumentException ex)

{

Console.WriteLine("Error: " + ex.Message);

throw; // Rethrow the exception for handling by the caller

}

}
```

2. Aggregate Exceptions: Use AggregateException to handle multiple exceptions that might occur within an asynchronous operation. Catch AggregateException to examine the inner exceptions and provide appropriate error handling.

Example:

```
async Task<int> PerformMultipleOperationsAsync()

{

try

{

// Perform multiple asynchronous operations

await Task.WhenAll(

Task.Run(() => DoOperation1()),

Task.Run(() => DoOperation2())

);

return 0; // Successful completion

}

catch (AggregateException ex)
```

```
{

foreach (var innerException in ex.InnerExceptions)

{

Console.WriteLine("Error: " + innerException.Message);

}

throw; // Rethrow the exception for handling by the caller

}

}
```

3. Task.Wait with Timeout: Use Task.Wait with a timeout to prevent indefinite waiting for a task to complete. Handle TimeoutException if the task doesn't complete within the specified timeout.

Example:

```
try

{

await task.Wait(TimeSpan.FromSeconds(5));

}

catch (TimeoutException ex)

{

Console.WriteLine("Operation timed out: " + ex.Message);

}
```

4. Task.ContinueWith: Use Task.ContinueWith to specify actions to be performed when a task completes or fails.

Example:

```
task.ContinueWith(t =>
```

```
{

if (t.IsFaulted)

{

Console.WriteLine("Task failed: " + t.Exception.Message);

}

else

{

Console.WriteLine("Task completed successfully.");

}

}, TaskContinuationOptions.OnlyOnFaulted);
```

How to cancel asynchronous operations?

In .NET, CancellationToken is used to provide a mechanism for cancel-ing asynchronous operations. It allows you to signal to an asynchronous task that it should be stopped.

Below are the Key Steps:

Create a CancellationTokenSource:using System.Threading;

```
CancellationTokenSource cts = new CancellationTokenSource();

CancellationToken token = cts.Token;
```

Pass the CancellationToken to the Asynchronous Method:async Task<int> CalculateFactorialAsync(int n, CancellationToken token)

```
{

// ...

}
```

Check for Cancellation Within the Method:if (token.IsCancellati onRequested)

{

throw new OperationCanceledException(token);

}

Cancel the Operation: cts.Cancel();

Example:

async Task Main()

{

using (CancellationTokenSource cts = new CancellationToken-Source())

{

CancellationToken token = cts.Token;

Task<int> task = CalculateFactorialAsync(5, token);

// Simulate cancellation after 2 seconds

await Task.Delay(2000, token);

cts.Cancel();

try

{

int result = await task;

Console.WriteLine($"Factorial of 5: {result}");

}

catch (OperationCanceledException ex)

{

```
Console.WriteLine("Operation canceled: " + ex.Message);

}

}

}
```

Important Considerations:

- **Cooperative Cancellation:** Asynchronous operations must be cooperative to respond to cancellation requests.

- **Timeout:** Use Task.WaitWithTimeout to set a timeout for asynchronous operations.

- **CancellationTokenSource.CancelAfter:** Use Cancellation TokenSource.CancelAfter to cancel after a specific delay.

- **Propagate Cancellation Tokens:** Pass CancellationToken to nested asynchronous calls to ensure proper cancellation propagation.

How to use ThreadPool for asynchronous operations?

A managed thread pool that provides a pool of worker threads for executing asynchronous tasks. Manages thread creation, scheduling, and recycling to optimize resource utilization. Offers a simple and efficient way to perform asynchronous operations.

Key Methods:

- **QueueUserWorkItem:** Queues a delegate for execution on a thread pool thread.

- **GetAvailableThreads:** Returns the number of available threads in the pool.

- **SetMaxThreads:** Sets the maximum number of threads in the pool.

Usage:

1. **Create a Delegate:** Define a delegate that represents the task you want to execute asynchronously.

2. **Queue the Delegate:** Use ThreadPool.QueueUserWorkItem to queue the delegate for execution.

3. **Handle Completion:** Optionally, use callbacks or events to handle the completion of the task.

Example:

```
using System.Threading;

void Main()

{

ThreadPool.QueueUserWorkItem(new WaitCallback(DoWork), "Hello from ThreadPool!");

}

void DoWork(object state)

{

Console.WriteLine(state);

Thread.Sleep(2000);

Console.WriteLine("Work completed.");

}
```

Key Points:

- **Thread Pool Management:** ThreadPool automatically manages the creation, scheduling, and recycling of threads.

- **Asynchronous Execution:** Tasks queued to the thread pool are executed asynchronously, allowing the main thread to continue with other tasks.

- **Thread Safety:** Ensure that your delegate is thread-safe if multiple threads will be accessing shared resources.

- **Limited Threads:** The ThreadPool has a limited number of threads. Avoid queuing too many tasks to prevent performance issues.

Additional Considerations:

- **Task-Based Asynchronous Pattern (TAP):** For more modern asynchronous programming, consider using the Task class and the async and await keywords.

- **SynchronizationContext:** If you need to update UI elements from a background thread, use SynchronizationContext to marshal the operation to the UI thread.

- **Cancellation:** Use CancellationToken to provide a way to cancel asynchronous operations.

What is the Callback in C#?

Callbacks are methods that are invoked by other methods or objects. They provide a way to define custom actions that can be executed asynchronously or in response to specific events.

Key Concepts:

- **Delegate:** A delegate is a type that represents a method with a specific signature. It's used to pass methods as arguments to other methods.

- **Event:** An event is a notification mechanism that allows objects to signal the occurrence of an event to other objects.

- **Callback Method:** A method that is invoked as a response to an event or as part of a callback mechanism.

Common Use Cases:

- **Event Handling:** Callback methods are commonly used as event handlers to respond to user actions or system events.

- **Asynchronous Operations:** Callbacks can be used to notify a caller when an asynchronous operation completes.

- **Customizable Behavior:** Callbacks can be used to provide customizable behavior within a library or framework.

Example:

```csharp
public delegate void MyCallback(string message);

public class MyClass

{

public event MyCallback OnEvent;

public void TriggerEvent()

{

if (OnEvent != null)

{

OnEvent("Event triggered!");

}

}

}

class Program

{

static void Main()

{

MyClass instance = new MyClass();

instance.OnEvent += HandleEvent;

instance.TriggerEvent();
```

```
}

static void HandleEvent(string message)

{

Console.WriteLine(message);

}

}
```

In this example:

1. A MyCallback delegate is defined to represent a method that takes a string as input.

2. The MyClass class defines an OnEvent event of type MyCallback.

3. The HandleEvent method is subscribed to the OnEvent event.

4. When the TriggerEvent method is called, the HandleEvent method is invoked as a callback.

Key Points:

- Callbacks can be implemented using delegates or lambda expressions.

- Callbacks can be used to decouple different parts of your code and make it more modular.

- Callbacks can be used to implement asynchronous operations and event-driven programming.

Give an example of an asynchronous callback with the help of a delegate.

```
using System;

using System.Threading.Tasks;
```

```csharp
public delegate void AsyncCallback(object sender, EventArgs e);

public class AsynchronousExample

{

public event AsyncCallback Completed;

public async Task PerformAsynchronousOperation()

{

await Task.Delay(2000); // Simulate a long-running task

if (Completed != null)

{

Completed(this, EventArgs.Empty);

}

}

}

class Program

{

static void Main()

{

AsynchronousExample example = new AsynchronousExample();

example.Completed += OnOperationCompleted;

example.PerformAsynchronousOperation();

}

static void OnOperationCompleted(object sender, EventArgs e)

{
```

Console.WriteLine("Asynchronous operation completed!");

}

}

In this example:

1. **AsyncCallback delegate:** This delegate defines a method that takes an object sender and EventArgs as input.

2. **AsynchronousExample class:** This class defines an OnEvent event of type AsyncCallback.

3. **PerformAsynchronousOperation method:** This method simulates a long-running asynchronous operation using Task .Delay.

4. **Event invocation:** If the Completed event is not null, it's invoked with the current instance of the AsynchronousExample class and an empty EventArgs object.

5. **Event handler:** The OnOperationCompleted method is subscribed to the Completed event and is executed when the event is triggered.

CHAPTER 3

.NET CORE HISTORY

.NET Core: A Journey of Evolution

NET Core, initially open-sourced by Microsoft, marked a significant departure from the monolithic .NET Framework. It introduced cross-platform capabilities, performance enhancements, and a modular architecture.

.NET Core 1.0 (Released June 27, 2016, End of Life: June 27, 2017)

- **Cross-platform:** Supported Windows, macOS, and Linux.

- **Modular design:** CoreCLR, ASP.NET Core, Entity Framework Core were separate components.

- **Performance improvements:** Enhanced startup time and throughput.

- **Cloud-native focus:** Optimized for cloud-based applications.

- **Command-line interface:** Introduced dotnet CLI for development and deployment.

.NET Core 1.1 (Released November 15, 2016, End of Life: November 15, 2017)

- **Performance enhancements:** Further improved startup time and throughput.

- **Expanded APIs:** Added support for more data types and features.

- **NuGet improvements:** Enhanced package management.

- **ASP.NET Core updates:** Added Razor Pages for simpler page-based development.

.NET Core 2.0 (Released May 27, 2017, End of Life: April 27, 2023)

- **Unified platform:** Merged ASP.NET Core into .NET Core.

- **Performance improvements:** Significant performance gains across the board.

- **New language features:** Introduced C# 7.0 features (pattern matching, tuples, etc.).

- **Entity Framework Core 2.0:** Enhanced database support and performance.

- **ASP.NET Core 2.0:** Added Razor Pages, SignalR, and other features.

.NET Core 2.1 (Released May 30, 2018, End of Life: February 21, 2022)

- **Performance optimizations:** Further improved startup time and throughput.

- **Generic Math class:** Added for mathematical operations.

- **Span<T>:** Introduced for low-level memory manipulation.

- **Blazor:** Introduced for building interactive web UIs with C#.

- **gRPC support:** Added for high-performance RPC communication.

.NET Core 2.2 (Released December 4, 2018, End of Life: April 23, 2022)

- **Performance enhancements:** Continued focus on performance improvements.

- **TLS 1.3 support:** Enhanced security.

- **Database providers:** Expanded support for database providers.

- **ASP.NET Core updates:** Added support for endpoint routing.

.NET Core 3.0 (Released September 23, 2019, End of Life: December 13, 2022)

- **Windows desktop support:** Enabled building Windows Forms and WPF applications.

- **Performance improvements:** Further optimized for performance.

- **C# 8.0:** Introduced new language features (nullable reference types, default interface methods, etc.).

- **Blazor WebAssembly:** Enabled client-side Blazor applications.

.NET 5 (Released November 10, 2020, End of Life: May 10, 2022)

- **Unified platform:** Merged .NET Core, .NET Framework, and Xamarin into a single platform.

- **Performance improvements:** Continued focus on performance.

- **C# 9.0:** Introduced new language features (top-level statements, records, etc.).

- **Single file applications:** Enabled self-contained deployments.

.NET 6 (Released November 8, 2021, End of Life: November 8, 2024)

- **Performance improvements:** Further optimized for performance.

- **C# 10:** Introduced new language features (file-scoped namespaces, interpolated strings, etc.).

- **Minimal APIs:** Simplified API development.

- **Hot Reload:** Enabled code changes without restarting the application.

.NET 7 (Released November 8, 2022, End of Life: May 8, 2025)

- **Performance improvements:** Continued focus on performance.

- **C# 11:** Introduced new language features (raw string literals, generic math, etc.).

- **Cloud-native enhancements:** Improved support for cloud-based applications.

- **Native AOT compilation:** Enabled smaller and faster applications.

Note: .NET has continued to evolve with subsequent releases, focusing on performance, developer experience, and cloud-native capabilities.

A Comprehensive Look at C# Versions

C# has evolved significantly since its inception, incorporating new features and paradigms to meet the evolving needs of developers. Let's delve into the key changes introduced with each version:

C# 1.0 (2000)

- The foundational version, introducing core object-oriented constructs: classes, structs, interfaces, inheritance, polymorphism, and properties.

- Emphasis on managed code execution and integration with the .NET Framework.

C# 2.0 (2005)

- **Generics:** Introduced to improve type safety and performance.

- **Partial classes:** Enabling code splitting across multiple files.

- **Iterators:** Simplified collection iteration.

- **Anonymous methods:** Facilitated delegate creation without explicit method declaration.

- **Nullable types:** Allowed for optional value types.

C# 3.0 (2007)

- **Language Integrated Query (LINQ):** Powerful query syntax for various data sources.

- **Lambda expressions:** Concise syntax for anonymous functions.

- **Extension methods:** Extending existing types without modifying them.

- **Implicitly typed local variables:** var keyword for automatic type inference.

- **Object and collection initializers:** Simplified object creation.

C# 4.0 (2010)

- **Dynamic typing:** Interoperability with dynamic languages.

- **Named and optional parameters:** Increased flexibility in method calls.

- **COM interop improvements:** Enhanced interaction with COM components.

- **Generic covariance and contravariance:** Improved type safety and flexibility.

C# 5.0 (2012)

- **Async/await:** Simplified asynchronous programming.

C# 6.0 (2015)

- **Expression-bodied members:** Concise syntax for methods, properties, and constructors.

- **Null-conditional operator:** Safe null handling.

- **String interpolation:** Enhanced string formatting.

- **Auto-property initializers:** Simplified property initialization.

- **Exception filters:** More granular exception handling.

C# 7.0 (2017)

- **Tuples:** Immutable value types for grouping data.

- **Pattern matching:** Improved type checking and conditional logic.

- **Local functions:** Nested functions within methods.

- **Ref locals and returns:** Improved performance in certain scenarios.

- **Out variables:** Simplified method arguments.

C# 8.0 (2019)

- **Nullable reference types:** Improved null safety.

- **Asynchronous streams:** Efficiently process asynchronous sequences.

- **Default interface methods:** Added default implementations to interfaces.

- **Pattern matching enhancements:** Expanded pattern matching capabilities.

- **Switch expressions:** Simplified switch statements.

C# 9.0 (2020)

- **Top-level statements:** Omitted Main method for simple programs.

- **Records:** Immutable data structures.

- **Init-only setters:** Restricted property modification after object creation.

- **Pattern matching improvements:** Enhanced pattern matching capabilities.

- **Covariant returns:** Allowed derived methods to return more specific types.

C# 10 (2022)

- **File-scoped namespaces:** Simplified namespace declarations.

- **Interpolated string handlers:** Custom formatting for interpolated strings.

- **Record structs:** Value-type records.

- **Structure types:** Improved performance and memory usage.

- **Extended property patterns:** Enhanced pattern matching with property access.

C# 11 (2022)

- **Raw string literals:** Simplified handling of multi-line strings.

- **Generic math:** Improved performance for generic math operations.

- **List patterns:** Enhanced pattern matching for lists.

- **Required members:** Guaranteed initialization of properties.

Note: C# continues to evolve with new features and improvements in subsequent versions.

.NET 8

.NET 8 represents a significant advancement over its predecessors, focusing on performance, developer experience, and cloud-native capabilities.

Key Improvements Over Previous Versions

- **Performance**: .NET 8 continues the relentless pursuit of performance optimization, building upon the gains achieved in .NET 6 and .NET 7. This includes improvements in startup time, throughput, and garbage collection.

- **Native AOT**: The introduction of native AOT compilation allows for the creation of smaller, faster, and self-contained applications, especially beneficial for containerized environments.

- **Cloud-Native Development**: .NET 8 further enhances support for cloud-native development with improvements in containerization, microservices, and serverless architectures.

- **Developer Productivity**: Features like hot reload and improved debugging experience enhance developer productivity.

- **C# 12**: Building on the foundation of C# 11, .NET 8 introduces new language features to streamline development and improve code readability.

- **ASP.NET Core**: Offers enhancements in Blazor, Minimal APIs, and overall performance.

- **Entity Framework Core**: Provides improvements in query performance, database providers, and features.

Specific Performance Enhancements:

- **Tiered Compilation**: Improved JIT compilation for better performance.

- **PGO (Profile-Guided Optimization)**: Enhanced performance based on runtime profile data.

- **Reduced garbage collection pauses**: Improved application responsiveness.

Additional Features:

- **Regular Expressions**: Significant performance improvements in regular expression matching.

- **JSON**: Faster JSON serialization and deserialization.

- **HTTP**: Enhanced HTTP client and server performance.

- **Native interop**: Improved interoperability with native code.

C# 12

C# 12 represents the latest evolution of the C# language, introducing several new features and enhancements that build upon the strengths of previous versions.

Key Features in C# 12

- **Primary Constructors**: This feature allows for a more concise and expressive way to define constructors, improving code readability.

- **Collection Expressions**: A new syntax for creating collections, providing a more fluent and expressive way to initialize collections.

- **Inline Arrays**: The ability to create arrays directly within a struct, enhancing performance and type safety.

- **Optional Parameters in Lambda Expressions**: Similar to method parameters, lambda expressions can now have optional parameters.

- **Ref readonly Parameters**: Improve clarity and safety when using ref parameters.

- Alias any type: Allows creating aliases for any type, not just named types.

- **Experimental attribute**: Indicates experimental features that might change in future versions.

- **Interceptors**: A preview feature for intercepting method calls.

CHAPTER 4

.NET CORE FUNDAMENTALS

What is .NET Core and how does it differ from the .NET Framework?

.NET Core is a free, open-source, cross-platform framework developed by Microsoft for building modern, cloud-based, and internet-connected applications. It is designed to be lightweight, modular, and high-performance, making it suitable for a wide range of applications, from web and mobile to microservices and IoT.

Here are some key differences between .NET Core and the .NET Framework:

1. **Cross-Platform Support**:

   ○ **.NET Core**: Runs on Windows, macOS, and Linux.

   ○ **.NET Framework**: Primarily runs on Windows.

2. **Open Source**:

   ○ **.NET Core**: Fully open-source with contributions from the community.

   ○ **.NET Framework**: Not fully open-source, though some components are available as open-source.

3. **Modular Architecture**:

- ○ **.NET Core**: Uses a modular architecture with NuGet packages, allowing developers to include only the libraries they need.

- ○ **.NET Framework**: Monolithic, with a larger set of libraries included by default.

4. **Performance**:

- ○ **.NET Core**: Optimized for performance and scalability, making it suitable for high-performance applications.

- ○ **.NET Framework**: While performant, it is not as optimized for modern, high-performance scenarios.

5. **Deployment**:

- ○ **.NET Core**: Supports side-by-side versioning, allowing multiple versions to coexist on the same machine.

- ○ **.NET Framework**: Typically installed system-wide, with version conflicts potentially affecting applications.

6. **Development Tools**:

- ○ **.NET Core**: Uses the .NET Core CLI for command-line development and supports Visual Studio Code, Visual Studio, and other editors.

- ○ **.NET Framework**: Primarily uses Visual Studio for development.

7. **Microservices and Containers**:

- ○ **.NET Core**: Well-suited for microservices architecture and containerized applications using Docker.

- ○ **.NET Framework**: Less optimized for microservices and containerization.

8. **API Surface**:

- ○ **.NET Core**: A subset of the .NET Framework API, with

        some APIs redesigned or removed for better performance and cross-platform compatibility.

        ◦ **.NET Framework**: A larger API surface with more legacy support.

These differences make .NET Core a more modern and flexible choice for new applications, especially those that need to run on multiple platforms or require high performance and scalability. However, the .NET Framework is still widely used for existing applications and enterprise environments that rely on its extensive libraries and Windows-specific features.

Explain the key features of .NET Core.

.NET Core is a cross-platform, high-performance, open-source framework for building modern applications. Here are some of its key features:

Cross-Platform Compatibility

- **Runs on Windows, macOS, and Linux:** .NET Core can be used to develop applications that run on a variety of operating systems, making it more flexible and adaptable.

- **Consistent Development Experience:** Developers can use the same tools and APIs across different platforms, improving productivity and reducing fragmentation.

Open-Source and Community-Driven

- **Community-Driven Development:** .NET Core is developed and maintained by a large and active community of developers, ensuring ongoing innovation and support.

- **Open-Source License:** The .NET Core framework is available under the MIT License, allowing for free use, distribution, and modification.

High-Performance

- **Optimized for Performance:** .NET Core is designed to deliver high performance and scalability, making it suitable for demanding workloads.

- **Just-In-Time (JIT) Compilation:** .NET Core uses JIT compilation to optimize code execution at runtime, improving performance.

Modern Application Development

- **ASP.NET Core:** A powerful framework for building web applications, APIs, and microservices.

- **Entity Framework Core:** An object-relational mapper (ORM) for data access.

- **Blazor:** A framework for building web applications using C# and HTML.

- **gRPC:** A high-performance RPC framework for building microservices.

Modular and Lightweight

- **Modular Architecture:** .NET Core is designed to be modular, allowing you to include only the components you need for your application.

- **Lightweight Footprint:** .NET Core has a smaller footprint compared to the .NET Framework, making it suitable for deployment on various environments, including cloud and IoT devices.

Side-by-Side Versions

- **Multiple Versions:** You can have multiple versions of .NET Core installed on the same machine without conflicts, enabling side-by-side deployment of different applications.

Integration with .NET Framework

- **Shared Codebase:** Many libraries and components are shared between .NET Core and the .NET Framework, allowing for easier migration and reuse of existing code.

These key features make .NET Core a versatile and powerful platform for building modern, cross-platform applications.

What platforms does .NET Core support?

.NET Core supports a wide range of platforms, making it a versatile framework for various development needs. Here are the primary platforms supported by .NET Core:

1. **Windows**: Full support for building and running applications.

2. **macOS**: Allows development and deployment of applications.

3. **Linux**: Supports multiple distributions, including Ubuntu, Debian, Fedora, and CentOS.

4. **iOS**: Through Xamarin, .NET Core can be used to build iOS applications.

5. **Android**: Also supported via Xamarin for building Android applications.

6. **WebAssembly (Wasm)**: Enables running .NET code in the browser.

7. **Docker:** .NET Core applications can be easily containerized using Docker for deployment to various environments.

Describe the architecture of .NET Core.

.NET Core is designed to be a highly modular and flexible framework. Its architecture consists of several key components:

CoreCLR (Common Language Runtime)

- **Execution Engine:** The CoreCLR is responsible for executing managed code, which is code written in languages like C#, F#, and VB.NET.

- **Garbage Collection:** It handles memory management through a garbage collector.

- **Type Safety:** Ensures type safety and security by verifying code at runtime.

.NET Core Libraries

- **Base Class Library (BCL):** Provides a rich set of classes for common programming tasks, such as collections, I/O, networking, and threading.

- **Additional Libraries:** .NET Core includes libraries for specific domains, such as ASP.NET Core for web development, Entity Framework Core for data access, and more.

.NET Core SDK

- **Tools and Libraries:** The SDK includes tools and libraries necessary for building, testing, and deploying .NET Core applications.

- **Command-Line Interface (CLI):** Provides a command-line interface for interacting with .NET Core projects and tools.

Host

- **Application Environment:** The host provides the environment in which .NET Core applications run, including configuration, logging, and dependency injection.

- **Hosting Models:** .NET Core supports various hosting models, such as self-hosting and hosting within IIS or Kestrel.

Application

- **User Code:** The application consists of your custom code written in a .NET Core-compatible language.

- **Dependencies:** It may rely on additional libraries or frameworks.

Key features of the architecture:

- **Modular design:** Components can be added or removed as needed.

- **Cross-platform:** Runs on Windows, macOS, and Linux.

- **High performance:** Optimized for performance and scalability.

- **Open-source:** Developed and maintained by a community of developers.

What are the main components of the .NET Core runtime?

The main components of the .NET Core runtime are:

- **CoreCLR (Common Language Runtime):** This is the execution engine that runs managed code, which is code written in languages like C#, F#, and VB.NET. It is responsible for tasks such as memory management, type safety, and code verification.

- **.NET Core Libraries:** These provide a rich set of classes for common programming tasks, such as collections, I/O, networking, and threading. They also include libraries for specific domains, such as ASP.NET Core for web development and Entity Framework Core for data access.

- **Host:** The host provides the environment in which .NET Core applications run, including configuration, logging, and dependency injection. It also handles the interaction with the operating system.

These components work together to provide a platform for running .NET Core applications.

Explain the implicit compilation process in .NET Core.

Implicit compilation in .NET Core refers to the automatic compilation of source code without requiring explicit compilation commands. This process is facilitated by the **Common Language Runtime (CLR)** and the **just-in-time (JIT) compiler**.

Here's how it works:

1. **Source Code:** When a .NET Core application is executed, the CLR loads the necessary assemblies (typically DLL files) containing the compiled code.

2. **JIT Compilation:** As the application runs, the JIT compiler analyzes the code and translates it into machine-specific instructions. This process is performed on a just-in-time basis, meaning the code is compiled only when it's actually needed.

3. **Execution:** Once the code is compiled, the CLR executes it.

4. **Caching:** The JIT compiler caches the compiled code to avoid recompiling it for subsequent calls. This improves performance.

Benefits of Implicit Compilation:

- **Faster Development:** Developers can focus on writing code without worrying about explicit compilation steps.

- **Dynamic Loading:** Assemblies can be loaded dynamically at runtime, allowing for more flexible application architectures.

- **Simplified Deployment:** Deploying .NET Core applications is often simpler, as only the compiled assemblies need to be distributed.

- **Platform Independence:** The CLR ensures that the compiled code can run on different platforms without requiring recompilation.

Key Points to Remember:

- Implicit compilation is a core feature of the .NET Core framework.

- The JIT compiler plays a crucial role in translating source code into machine-specific instructions.

- The CLR manages the loading and execution of assemblies.

- Implicit compilation can improve development efficiency and deployment simplicity.

How does .NET Core handle memory management?

.NET Core handles memory management primarily through its **Garbage Collector (GC)**, which is an automatic memory management system. Here are the key aspects of how it works:

Managed Heap: .NET Core applications allocate memory from a managed heap. The heap is divided into segments, and objects are allocated contiguously within these segments.

Generations: The managed heap is divided into three generations: Generation 0, Generation 1, and Generation 2. This generational approach helps optimize garbage collection:

Generation 0: Contains short-lived objects. These objects are collected frequently.

Generation 1: Serves as a buffer between short-lived and long-lived objects.

Generation 2: Contains long-lived objects. These objects are collected less frequently.

Garbage Collection Process: The GC periodically checks for objects that are no longer referenced by the application. When it finds such objects, it reclaims their memory, making it available for future allocations.

The GC operates in different modes (e.g., workstation, server) to balance performance and responsiveness based on the application's needs.

Large Object Heap (LOH): Objects larger than 85,000 bytes are allocated in the Large Object Heap. The LOH is collected less frequently than the small object heap to reduce fragmentation.

Automatic Memory Management: Developers do not need to manually allocate or free memory. The GC handles these tasks, reducing the risk of memory leaks and other memory-related issues.

Performance Optimization: The GC is optimized to minimize pauses and improve application performance.It uses techniques like background garbage collection to perform collections without significantly impacting application responsiveness.

Memory Analysis Tools: .NET Core provides tools like dotnet-trace and Visual Studio's diagnostic tools to analyze memory usage, detect memory leaks, and optimize memory management[1].

These features make .NET Core's memory management robust and efficient, allowing developers to focus on building applications without worrying about low-level memory management details.

What is the .NET Core CLI and how is it used?

The **.NET Core Command-Line Interface (CLI)** is a powerful tool that provides a command-line interface for interacting with .NET Core projects and tools. It allows you to perform various tasks without the need for a full-featured IDE, making it a valuable tool for developers who prefer to work from the command line.

Key features of the .NET Core CLI:

- **Project creation:** Create new .NET Core projects of different types (e.g., console applications, web applications, class libraries).

- **Building and running:** Build your projects into executable files and run them.

- **NuGet package management:** Install, uninstall, and update NuGet packages.

- **Testing:** Run unit tests and integration tests.

- **Publishing:** Publish your applications for deployment.

- **Debugging:** Debug your applications using the built-in debugger.

- **Scaffolding:** Generate code snippets for common tasks, such as creating controllers, views, and models.

Basic usage:

1. **Open a terminal or command prompt.**

2. **Navigate to the directory where you want to create your project.**

3. **Use the dotnet new command to create a new project:**dotnet new console -o MyProject

This will create a new console application project named "MyProject".

4. Run the project:dotnet run

This will compile and run your project.

Additional commands:

- **dotnet restore:** Restores NuGet packages for your project.

- **dotnet build:** Builds your project into an assembly.

- **dotnet publish:** Publishes your project for deployment.

- **dotnet test:** Runs unit tests in your project.

- **dotnet clean:** Removes intermediate build files.

Explain the concept of cross-platform development in .NET Core.

Cross-platform development in .NET Core refers to the ability to create applications that can run on multiple operating systems, such as Windows, macOS, and Linux. This is made possible by the .NET Core framework's **modular architecture** and its use of the **CoreCLR** (Common Language Runtime), which is designed to be portable across different platforms.

Key benefits of cross-platform development in .NET Core:

- **Code reusability:** Developers can write a single codebase that can be deployed to multiple platforms, reducing development time and maintenance costs.

- **Expanded reach:** Applications can be made available to a wider audience by supporting multiple operating systems.

- **Flexibility:** Developers can choose the platform that best suits their needs and preferences.

- **Consistency:** .NET Core provides a consistent development experience across different platforms, making it easier for developers to learn and use.

How cross-platform development works in .NET Core:

1. **Single codebase:** Developers write their applications using C#, F#, or other .NET languages.

2. **.NET Core SDK:** The .NET Core SDK is used to build and run the application.

3. **CoreCLR:** The CoreCLR is responsible for executing the application code on the target platform.

4. **Platform-specific libraries:** .NET Core includes platform-specific libraries that provide access to features like file I/O, networking, and graphics. These libraries are designed to abstract away the differences between platforms, allowing developers to write platform-agnostic code.

Explain the concept of the Base Class Library (BCL) in .NET Core.

The **Base Class Library (BCL)** in .NET Core is a fundamental component that provides a comprehensive set of classes and types for common programming tasks. It serves as the foundation for building .NET Core applications and offers a wide range of functionalities.

Key features of the BCL:

- **Core data types:** Includes fundamental data types like int, string, bool, decimal, and DateTime.

- **Collections:** Provides various collection classes for storing and manipulating data, such as List, Dictionary, HashSet, and Queue.

- **IO operations:** Offers classes for reading from and writing to files, streams, and other sources of data.

- **Networking:** Provides classes for network communication, including TCP/IP sockets, HTTP clients, and web services.

- **Reflection:** Allows you to dynamically inspect and manipulate types and their members at runtime.

- **Threading and tasks:** Provides classes for creating and managing threads and asynchronous operations.

- **Security:** Offers classes for cryptographic operations, authentication, and authorization.

- **XML and JSON:** Includes support for working with XML and JSON data.

- **Regular expressions:** Provides classes for matching and manipulating text patterns.

Benefits of using the BCL:

- **Productivity:** The BCL provides a rich set of pre-built classes, saving developers time and effort.

- **Consistency:** The BCL ensures consistent behavior across different platforms and applications.

- **Performance:** The BCL is optimized for performance, providing efficient implementations of common tasks.

- **Cross-platform compatibility:** The BCL is designed to be compatible with various .NET Core platforms, including Windows, macOS, and Linux.

What is the IGCToCLR interface?

The **IGCToCLR interface** is a crucial component in the .NET runtime that bridges the gap between the **garbage collector (GC)** and the **Common Language Runtime (CLR)**. It plays a pivotal role in managing memory allocation and deallocation within .NET applications.

Key functions of the IGCToCLR interface:

- **Notification of GC Events:** The GC uses IGCToCLR to notify the CLR about various events, such as when a GC collection is about to start or when a collection has completed. This allows the CLR to take appropriate actions, such as suspending threads or releasing resources.

- **Providing Information to the GC:** The CLR can provide information to the GC through IGCToCLR, such as the addresses of objects that need to be collected or the types of objects that are eligible for collection. This helps the GC make informed decisions about which objects to prioritize.

- **Handling GC-Induced Exceptions:** When a GC collection occurs, it can sometimes lead to exceptions, such as OutOfMemoryException. The IGCToCLR interface allows the CLR to handle these exceptions and take appropriate actions, such as notifying the application or terminating the process.

Why is IGCToCLR important?

- **Efficient Memory Management:** By effectively communicating between the GC and the CLR, IGCToCLR helps ensure that memory is allocated and deallocated efficiently, preventing memory leaks and improving application performance.

- **Safe Execution:** IGCToCLR helps the CLR handle GC-induced exceptions gracefully, preventing unexpected application termination.

- **Platform Independence:** IGCToCLR is a core part of the .NET runtime and is implemented consistently across different platforms, ensuring that .NET applications behave predictably regardless of the underlying operating system.

What is the role of NuGet packages in .NET Core development?

NuGet packages play a crucial role in .NET Core development by providing a convenient way to share and reuse code libraries. They are essentially compressed files that contain a collection of assemblies, source code, and other resources.

Key benefits of using NuGet packages:

- **Code reusability:** By using NuGet packages, developers can leverage existing code libraries without having to write everything from scratch. This saves time and effort.

- **Dependency management:** NuGet packages help manage dependencies between different parts of your application. You can easily add, remove, and update packages using the NuGet package manager.

- **Community contributions:** NuGet is a large and active community where developers share their code libraries. This means you have access to a vast ecosystem of packages for various purposes.

- **Ease of installation:** Installing NuGet packages is simple. You can use the NuGet package manager in Visual Studio or the dotnet CLI to add packages to your project.

How NuGet packages work:

1. **Package creation:** Developers create NuGet packages by packaging their code libraries and metadata into a .nupkg file.

2. **Package publication:** The package is then published to a NuGet feed, which is a repository of NuGet packages.

3. **Package consumption:** Developers can search for and install NuGet packages from the feed using the NuGet package manager. The package is added to the project's dependencies, and

its assemblies are referenced in the application's code.

Popular NuGet packages:

- **Microsoft.Extensions.DependencyInjection:** Provides dependency injection services.

- **Microsoft.AspNetCore:** A framework for building web applications and APIs.

- **Newtonsoft.Json:** A popular JSON serializer.

- **NUnit:** A unit testing framework.

- **FluentValidation:** A framework for validating objects.

What is MEF in .NET Core?

MEF (Managed Extensibility Framework) is a component model in .NET Core that allows you to dynamically discover, compose, and extend applications. It provides a flexible and extensible way to build modular applications where different components can be added or removed without recompiling the entire application.

Key Features of MEF:

- **Composable Parts:** MEF defines a **part** as a class that can be composed into a larger application. Parts can export services or import services from other parts.

- **Catalogs:** A **catalog** is a collection of parts that can be discovered and composed. MEF provides built-in catalogs for discovering parts from assemblies, directories, and other sources.

- **Composition Engine:** The **composition engine** is responsible for creating instances of parts and wiring them together based on their import and export contracts. It uses metadata attributes to determine how parts should be composed.

- **Metadata Attributes:** MEF uses **metadata attributes** to describe the import and export contracts of parts. These attributes provide information about the type of service a part exports or imports.

How to Use MEF in .NET Core:

1. **Define Parts:** Create classes that represent the parts you want to compose. Use the [Export] attribute to export services and the [Import] attribute to import services.

2. **Create a Catalog:** Use a catalog to discover the parts in your application. Common catalogs include DirectoryCatalog, AssemblyCatalog, and AggregateCatalog.

3. **Compose the Application:** Create a composition container and add the catalogs to it. Use the container's ComposeParts method to create instances of the parts and wire them together based on their import and export contracts.

Example:

```
using System.ComponentModel.Composition;

using System.ComponentModel.Composition.Hosting;

namespace MEFExample

{

[Export]

public class Calculator

{

[Import]

public IAdditionService AdditionService { get; set; }

public int Add(int a, int b)

{

return AdditionService.Add(a, b);

}
```

```csharp
}
[Export(typeof(IAdditionService))]
public class AdditionServiceImplementation : IAdditionService
{
public int Add(int a, int b)
{
return a + b;
}
}
public interface IAdditionService
{
int Add(int a, int b);
}
public class Program
{
public static void Main()
{
var catalog = new AssemblyCatalog(typeof(Program).Assembly);
var container = new CompositionContainer(catalog);
var calculator = container.GetExportedValue<Calculator>();
var result = calculator.Add(5, 8);
Console.WriteLine(result);
}
```

```
}

}
```

In this example, the Calculator part imports an IAdditionService and uses it to perform addition. The AdditionServiceImplementation class exports an IAdditionService and provides the actual implementation. The MEF composition engine automatically wires these parts together based on their import and export contracts.

How do you deploy a .NET Core application?

Deploying a .NET Core application involves several steps to make it accessible to users. Here's a general overview of the process:

1. Choose a Deployment Method:

- **Self-hosted:** Deploy the application on your own server or infrastructure.

- **Cloud-based:** Utilize cloud platforms like Azure, AWS, or Google Cloud for hosting.

- **Containerization:** Package the application into a container (e.g., Docker) for portability and scalability.

2. Prepare the Application:

- **Build and publish:** Create the deployment artifacts, which typically include compiled assemblies, configuration files, and dependencies.

- **Configure settings:** Set up necessary configuration settings for the deployment environment, such as database connections, API keys, and logging levels.

3. Deploy to the Target Environment:

- **Copy files:** Transfer the deployment artifacts to the target server or cloud platform.

- **Configure the environment:** Set up the necessary environment variables and dependencies on the target machine.

- **Start the application:** Run the application's entry point to start it.

Specific Deployment Scenarios:

- **Self-hosted:**

  - Copy the published files to a web server (e.g., IIS, Kestrel).

  - Configure the web server to serve the application.

- **Cloud-based:**

  - Use the cloud platform's deployment tools (e.g., Azure App Service, AWS Elastic Beanstalk) to deploy the application.

  - Configure the cloud platform's settings according to your needs.

- **Containerization:**

  - Build a Docker image containing your application and its dependencies.

  - Push the image to a container registry (e.g., Docker Hub).

  - Run the container on a container orchestration platform (e.g., Kubernetes, Docker Swarm).

How do you handle configuration in .NET Core?

.NET Core provides a flexible and extensible configuration system that allows you to manage application settings in a structured and organized manner. This system supports various configuration sources, such as environment variables, appsettings.json files, command-line arguments, and user secrets.

Key components of the configuration system:

- **IConfiguration:** This is the main interface for accessing configuration values. It provides methods for reading values of different data types.

- **IConfigurationBuilder:** This class is used to build the configuration object by adding different configuration sources.

- **Configuration providers:** These are responsible for reading configuration values from specific sources, such as environment variables, appsettings.json files, and user secrets.

Common configuration sources:

- **Environment variables:** Key-value pairs defined in the environment where the application runs.

- **Appsettings.json:** A JSON file that contains configuration settings.

- **Command-line arguments:** Values passed to the application when it is started.

- **User secrets:** Sensitive configuration values that are stored securely.

- **Configuration providers:** Custom providers can be created to read configuration values from other sources, such as Azure Key Vault or database.

Example:

```
using Microsoft.Extensions.Configuration;

var builder = new ConfigurationBuilder()

.SetBasePath(Directory.GetCurrentDirectory())

.AddJsonFile("appsettings.json", optional: true, reloadOnChange: true)

.AddEnvironmentVariables();

var configuration = builder.Build();

var connectionString = configuration.GetConnectionString("MyCon
nectionString");
```

```
var apiUrl = configuration["ApiUrl"];
```

Key features of the configuration system:

- **Hierarchical configuration:** Configuration values can be organized into sections and subsections.

- **Type safety:** The system provides strong typing for configuration values, preventing errors and improving code readability.

- **Configuration binding:** You can bind configuration values to strongly typed objects for easier access and validation.

- **Environment-specific configuration:** You can create different configuration files for different environments (e.g., development, staging, production) and load the appropriate configuration based on the environment.

- **Dependency injection:** The configuration system integrates well with dependency injection, allowing you to inject configuration values into your services.

What are the benefits of using SignalR in .NET Core applications, and how does it differ from traditional AJAX-based communication?

SignalR is a library that simplifies real-time communication in .NET Core applications. It provides a high-level API for building features such as:

- **Real-time updates:** SignalR allows you to push content to connected clients without requiring them to poll the server for changes. This is especially useful for applications that need to display data that changes frequently, such as chat applications, online games, and dashboards.

- **Server-side push:** SignalR enables server-side push, meaning the server can initiate communication with the client at any time. This is in contrast to traditional HTTP requests, where the client always initiates the communication.

- **Scalability:** SignalR can handle a large number of concurrent connections, making it suitable for high-traffic applications.

- **Cross-platform support:** SignalR works with a variety of clients, including web browsers, mobile devices, and desktop applications.

- **Simplified development:** SignalR provides a high-level API that abstracts away the complexities of real-time communication, making it easier to develop real-time features in your .NET Core applications.

Differences Between SignalR and Traditional AJAX-based Communication

Communication initiation	Client-initiated	Server-initiated
Update frequency	Periodic polling	Real-time push
Efficiency	Less efficient	More efficient
Scalability	It can be challenging for large numbers of clients	Well-suited for large numbers of clients

Traditional AJAX-based communication involves the client periodically polling the server for updates. This can be inefficient, especially for applications that need to display data that changes frequently.

SignalR, on the other hand, uses a server-side push mechanism that allows the server to initiate communication with the client as needed. This results in a more efficient and responsive user experience.

Here's a table summarizing the key differences:

What is dependency injection and how is it implemented in .NET Core?

Dependency Injection (DI) is a software design pattern that promotes loose coupling between classes by passing dependencies (objects that a class needs to function) into the class rather than having the class create them itself. This makes the code more modular, testable, and maintainable.

In .NET Core, DI is a core principle and is implemented through the **Microsoft.Extensions.DependencyInjection** package. This package provides a simple and flexible way to register dependencies and inject them into classes that need them.

Key concepts of DI in .NET Core:

- **Service:** A class or interface that provides a service to other classes.

- **Client:** A class that consumes a service.

- **Dependency:** A service that a client needs to function.

- **Dependency Injection Container:** A component that manages the lifecycle of services and injects them into clients.

Implementation steps:

1. **Register services:** Use the IServiceCollection interface to register services with the dependency injection container. You can register concrete classes or interfaces.

2. **Build the service provider:** Call the BuildServiceProvider() method on the IServiceCollection to create the service provider.

3. **Resolve services:** Use the service provider to resolve services from the container. You can resolve services by type or by name.

Example:

```
using Microsoft.Extensions.DependencyInjection;
```

```csharp
public interface IGreetingService

{

string SayHello(string name);

}

public class GreetingService : IGreetingService

{

public string SayHello(string name) => $"Hello, {name}!";

}

public class Program

{

public static void Main(string[] args)

{

var services = new ServiceCollection();

services.AddTransient<IGgreetingService, GreetingService>();

var serviceProvider = services.BuildServiceProvider();

var greetingService = serviceProvider.GetRequiredService<IGgreeting
Service>();

Console.WriteLine(greetingService.SayHello("World"));

}

}
```

In this example:

- IGgreetingService is an interface defining the SayHello method.

- GreetingService is a concrete implementation of the IGgreet-ingService interface.

- The services.AddTransient<IGgreetingService, GreetingService>(); line registers the GreetingService as a transient service, meaning a new instance will be created each time it is requested.

- The serviceProvider.GetRequiredService<IGgreetingService>(); line resolves the IGgreetingService from the service provider.

Benefits of using DI in .NET Core:

- **Loose coupling:** Classes are less tightly coupled, making them easier to test, maintain, and reuse.

- **Testability:** DI makes it easier to write unit tests by injecting mock or stub implementations of dependencies.

- **Modularity:** Code is more modular and easier to understand.

- **Dependency management:** The DI container manages the lifecycle of dependencies, reducing the need for manual management.

How does .NET Core support microservices architecture?

.NET Core provides a strong foundation for building microservices architectures. Its modular design, performance, and cross-platform capabilities make it well-suited for developing and deploying microservices.

Here are some key ways .NET Core supports microservices:

1. Modular Architecture:

- **Small, independent services:** .NET Core's modular design allows you to break down large applications into smaller, independent services, each with its own responsibilities.

- **Loose coupling:** Services can communicate with each other through well-defined APIs, reducing dependencies and improving maintainability.

2. Performance and Scalability:

- **Optimized for performance:** .NET Core is designed to be efficient and performant, making it suitable for handling high-traffic microservices.

- **Scalability:** Microservices can be scaled independently based on demand, ensuring optimal resource utilization.

3. Cross-Platform Compatibility:

- **Deploy anywhere:** Microservices built with .NET Core can be deployed on various platforms, including Windows, macOS, and Linux. This provides flexibility and allows you to choose the best hosting environment for each service.

4. Cloud-Native Support:

- **Containerization:** .NET Core integrates well with container- ization technologies like Docker, making it easy to package and deploy microservices as containers.

- **Cloud platforms:** .NET Core is compatible with major cloud platforms like Azure, AWS, and Google Cloud, providing a range of services for hosting and managing microservices.

5. ASP.NET Core:

- **Web API framework:** ASP.NET Core is a powerful frame- work for building RESTful APIs, which are essential for mi- croservices communication.

- **Lightweight and performant:** ASP.NET Core is designed to be lightweight and efficient, making it suitable for microser- vices.

6. gRPC:

- **High-performance RPC:** gRPC is a high-performance RPC framework that can be used for communication between mi- croservices. It offers efficient serialization and transport, mak- ing it ideal for demanding workloads.

7. Service Discovery:

- **Service registration and discovery:** Tools like Consul or Kubernetes can be used to register and discover microservices, making it easier to manage and scale them.

8. Configuration Management:

- **Centralized configuration:** .NET Core provides tools for managing configuration settings across microservices, ensuring consistency and flexibility.

How does .NET Core ensure application security?

.NET Core provides a robust set of features to ensure application security. Here are some key mechanisms:

1. Authentication and Authorization:

- **ASP.NET Core Identity:** Built-in membership and authentication system for managing user accounts, roles, and permissions.

- **OAuth and OpenID Connect:** Support for industry-standard protocols for external authentication providers (e.g. , Google, Facebook).

- **Authorization policies:** Define rules for granting or denying access to resources based on user roles, claims, or custom conditions.

2. Input Validation and Sanitization:

- **Model binding:** Automatically maps incoming data to strongly typed models, providing validation and sanitization.

- **Data annotations:** Apply attributes to model properties to enforce validation rules (e.g., required, data type, range).

- **Custom validation:** Create custom validation logic to address specific requirements.

3. Cross-Site Request Forgery (CSRF) Protection:

- **Token-based approach:** Generate a unique token for each request and verify it on the server to prevent unauthorized requests.

4. Cross-Site Scripting (XSS) Prevention:

- **Output encoding:** Encode output to prevent malicious scripts from being executed.

- **Content Security Policy (CSP):** Define rules to restrict the resources that can be loaded by the browser.

5. SQL Injection Prevention:

- **Parameterized queries:** Use parameterized queries to prevent SQL injection attacks.

- **ORM frameworks:** Entity Framework Core provides built-in protection against SQL injection.

6. Secure Communication:

- **HTTPS:** Use HTTPS to encrypt communication between the client and server.

- **TLS/SSL:** Implement strong encryption protocols to protect sensitive data.

7. Dependency Injection:

- **Loose coupling:** Dependency injection promotes loose coupling, making it easier to isolate and replace components if vulnerabilities are discovered.

What is Kestrel and how does it fit into the ASP.NET Core architecture?

Kestrel is the **default web server** for ASP.NET Core applications. It's a lightweight, cross-platform server optimized for performance and efficiency. Here's how it fits into the ASP.NET Core architecture:

ASP.NET Core Application Workflow:

1. **Client Request:** A user interacts with your web application through a web browser, sending an HTTP request.

2. **Kestrel:** Kestrel listens for incoming HTTP requests on a specific port (usually port 5000 by default).

3. **Processing Request:** When a request arrives, Kestrel parses it and creates an HttpContext object containing information about the request, like headers, body, and cookies.

4. **ASP.NET Core Pipeline:** Kestrel then hands off the HttpContext object to the ASP.NET Core pipeline.

5. **Middleware Processing:** The request goes through a series of middleware components in the pipeline. These components can perform tasks like authentication, authorization, routing, and logging.

6. **Application Logic:** The middleware eventually routes the request to the appropriate controller action in your application code.

7. **Response Generation:** Your application logic processes the request, generates a response (HTML, JSON, etc.), and sends it back to the pipeline.

8. **Kestrel Response:** Kestrel receives the response from the pipeline, formats it as an HTTP response, and sends it back to the client's web browser.

Benefits of Kestrel:

Cross-Platform: Kestrel runs on Windows, Linux, and macOS, making it suitable for various deployment environments.

Performance: Kestrel is designed for high performance, offering efficient handling of concurrent connections.

Lightweight: Kestrel has a small footprint, making it ideal for resource-constrained environments like containers.

Security: Kestrel supports HTTPS and is hardened against web server vulnerabilities.

Simplicity: Kestrel is easily configurable and requires minimal setup for basic functionality.

Important Note:

While Kestrel is the default, it's not mandatory. You can use ASP.N ET Core applications behind a reverse proxy server like IIS, Nginx, or Apache for additional features like load balancing and advanced security configurations. In these cases, Kestrel still handles the HTTP requests received from the reverse proxy.

What are the differences between .Net Core and Mono?

Both .NET Core and Mono are implementations of the .NET framework, providing a platform for developing applications using C# and other .NET languages. However, they have some key differences:

1. Origin:

- **.NET Core:** Created and maintained by Microsoft.

- **Mono:** Initially developed by Novell (now part of Micro Focus) and later supported by the Xamarin community.

2. Platform Support:

- **.NET Core:** Originally focused on cross-platform support for Windows, Linux, and macOS. It's now fully integrated into the .NET platform.

- **Mono:** Primarily focused on cross-platform support for Unix-like systems, including Linux, macOS, and BSD.

3. Performance:

- **.NET Core:** Generally considered to have better performance than Mono due to optimizations and direct integration with the underlying operating system.

- **Mono:** Has made significant performance improvements over the years but may still lag slightly behind .NET Core in certain scenarios.

4. Ecosystem and Community:

- **.NET Core:** Has a larger and more active community, benefiting from Microsoft's support and integration with Visual Studio.

- **Mono:** Has a strong community, especially around mobile development with Xamarin.

5. Future:

- **.NET Core:** Is the primary focus of Microsoft's .NET development efforts and is the recommended platform for most new applications.

- **Mono:** While still maintained, its development is less active compared to .NET Core. It's primarily used for legacy applications and specific scenarios where .NET Core might not be suitable.

CHAPTER 5

ASP.NET CORE

What is the difference between .NET Core and ASP. NET Core?

The key difference between .NET Core and ASP.NET Core lies in their purpose:

1. .NET Core:

- **General-purpose framework:** .NET Core is a **free and open-source** framework that provides a foundation for building various types of applications, including console applications, web services, libraries, and more.

- **Cross-platform:** Runs on Windows, macOS, and Linux, offering flexibility for deployment.

- **Modular design:** Consists of libraries and tools that can be added or removed depending on application needs.

- **Focus on performance and scalability:** Optimized for efficient execution and handling high-traffic applications.

Think of .NET Core as a toolbox containing various tools for building different kinds of software.

2. ASP.NET Core:

- **Web-specific framework:** ASP.NET Core is a **web applica-

tion framework built on top of .NET Core. It provides tools and libraries specifically designed for building web applications and APIs (Application Programming Interfaces).

- **Focuses on web development:** Features like routing, middleware, controllers, and views cater to the specific needs of web applications.

- **Inherits benefits from .NET Core:** ASP.NET Core benefits from .NET Core's cross-platform compatibility, performance, and modular design.

In summary:

- **.NET Core** provides the foundation upon which ASP.NET Core is built.

- **ASP.NET Core** extends .NET Core with features specifically for web development.

When to choose which:

- If you need to build a console application, library, or non-web service, use .NET Core.

- If you're building a web application or web API, use ASP.NET Core.

Explain the concept of middleware in ASP.NET Core.

Middleware in ASP.NET Core is a software component that is assembled into an application pipeline to handle requests and responses. Each middleware component in the pipeline can:

1. **Process an incoming request**.

2. **Decide whether to pass the request to the next component** in the pipeline.

3. **Perform actions before and after the next component** in the pipeline.

Key Concepts of Middleware

1. Request Delegates:

- Middleware components are built using request delegates, which handle each HTTP request.

- Request delegates are configured using Run, Map, and Use extension methods.

2. Middleware Pipeline:

- The middleware pipeline is a sequence of middleware components that are executed in the order they are added.

- Each component can perform operations both before and after the next component in the pipeline.

3. Terminal Middleware:

- A middleware component that does not call the next middleware is called terminal middleware. It short-circuits the pipeline and prevents further processing.

Example of Middleware in ASP.NET Core

Here's a simple example of how to set up middleware in an ASP.NET Core application:

Creating a Middleware Component:

```
public class CustomMiddleware

{

private readonly RequestDelegate _next;

public CustomMiddleware(RequestDelegate next)

{

_next = next;
```

```
}

public async Task InvokeAsync(HttpContext context)

{

// Do something before the next middleware

await context.Response.WriteAsync("Hello from Custom Middleware!
\n");

// Call the next middleware in the pipeline

await _next(context);

// Do something after the next middleware

}

}
```

Registering Middleware in the Pipeline:

```
public class Startup

{

public void Configure(IApplicationBuilder app, IWebHostEnvironment env)

{

app.UseMiddleware<CustomMiddleware>();

app.Run(async context =>

{

await context.Response.WriteAsync("Hello from Terminal Middleware!\n");

});

}
```

}

In this example, CustomMiddleware writes a message to the response before and after calling the next middleware. The Run method is used to add terminal middleware that handles the request and produces a response.

Common Middleware Components

ASP.NET Core includes many built-in middleware components for handling tasks such as:

- **Authentication**: Validating user credentials.

- **Authorization**: Checking user permissions.

- **Logging**: Recording request and response details.

- **Error Handling**: Managing exceptions and errors.

- **Static Files**: Serving static files like HTML, CSS, and JavaScript.

What is dependency injection and how is it implemented in ASP.NET Core?

Dependency Injection (DI) is a design pattern used to achieve Inversion of Control (IoC) between classes and their dependencies. Instead of a class creating its own dependencies, they are injected from the outside, typically through constructor parameters. This promotes loose coupling and makes the code more modular, testable, and maintainable.

How Dependency Injection Works in ASP.NET Core

ASP.NET Core has built-in support for dependency injection. Here's a step-by-step guide on how it is implemented:

Define Interfaces and Implementations:

1. Create an interface that defines the contract for your service.

2. Implement the interface in a class.

```
public interface IMyService

{

void DoWork();

}

public class MyService : IMyService

{

public void DoWork()

{

// Implementation code

}

}
```

Register Services with the DI Container:

1. Register your services in the ConfigureServices method of the Startup class or in the Program.cs file.

```
public void ConfigureServices(IServiceCollection services)

{

services.AddTransient<IMyService, MyService>();

}
```

1. Here, AddTransient specifies that a new instance of MyService will be created each time it is requested. Other lifetimes include AddScoped (one instance per request) and AddSingleton (one instance for the entire application).

Inject Services into Controllers or Other Classes: Use constructor injection to get the service instance.

```
public class MyController : Controller
```

```
{

private readonly IMyService _myService;

public MyController(IMyService myService)

{

_myService = myService;

}

public IActionResult Index()

{

_myService.DoWork();

return View();

}

}
```

Benefits of Dependency Injection

- **Loose Coupling**: Classes are not tightly bound to their dependencies.

- **Easier Testing**: Dependencies can be mocked or stubbed during unit testing.

- **Improved Maintainability**: Changes to dependencies require minimal changes to the classes that use them.

How do you configure services in an ASP.NET Core application?

Configuring services in an ASP.NET Core application involves registering services with the dependency injection (DI) container. This is typically done in the ConfigureServices method of the Startup class or in the Program.cs file. Here's a step-by-step guide:

Step-by-Step Guide to Configuring Services

1. Create the Service Interface and Implementation:

- Define an interface for your service.

- Implement the interface in a class.

```
public interface IMyService

{

void DoWork();

}

public class MyService : IMyService

{

public void DoWork()

{

// Implementation code

}

}
```

1. Register the Service with the DI Container:

- Register your service in the ConfigureServices method or in the Program.cs file.

```
public class Startup

{

public void ConfigureServices(IServiceCollection services)

{

services.AddTransient<IMyService, MyService>();
```

}

}

In the Program.cs file, it would look like this:var builder = WebApplic ation.CreateBuilder(args);

builder.Services.AddTransient<IMyService, MyService>();

var app = builder.Build();

Here, AddTransient specifies that a new instance of MyService will be created each time it is requested. Other lifetimes include AddScoped (one instance per request) and AddSingleton (one instance for the entire application).

1. **Inject the Service into Controllers or Other Classes**:

- Use constructor injection to get the service instance.

public class MyController : Controller

{

private readonly IMyService _myService;

public MyController(IMyService myService)

{

_myService = myService;

}

public IActionResult Index()

{

_myService.DoWork();

return View();

}

}

Common Service Lifetimes

- **Transient**: Created each time they are requested.

- **Scoped**: Created once per request.

- **Singleton**: Created once and shared throughout the application's lifetime.

Example of Configuring Multiple Services

You can register multiple services in the ConfigureServices method:

```
public void ConfigureServices(IServiceCollection services)

{

services.AddTransient<IMyService, MyService>();

services.AddScoped<IOtherService, OtherService>();

services.AddSingleton<IAnotherService, AnotherService>();

}
```

Benefits of Configuring Services

- **Loose Coupling**: Classes are not tightly bound to their dependencies.

- **Easier Testing**: Dependencies can be mocked or stubbed during unit testing.

- **Improved Maintainability**: Changes to dependencies require minimal changes to the classes that use them.

What is the purpose of the Startup class in ASP.NET Core?

The **Startup class** in ASP.NET Core is essential for configuring the application's services and the request processing pipeline. It acts as the entry point for the application and is responsible for setting up everything needed for the app to run.

Key Responsibilities of the Startup Class

   1. **ConfigureServices Method**:

- This method is used to register services with the dependency injection (DI) container. Services are reusable components that provide functionality to the application.

- You can add services like database contexts, logging, authentication, and more.

```
public void ConfigureServices(IServiceCollection services)

{

services.AddControllersWithViews();

services.AddDbContext<MyDbContext>(options =>

options.UseSqlServer(Configuration.GetConnectionString("DefaultConnection")));

}
```

   1. **Configure Method**:

- This method is used to define the middleware pipeline. Middleware components handle HTTP requests and responses.

- You can add middleware for tasks like error handling, static file serving, routing, and more.

```
public void Configure(IApplicationBuilder app, IWebHostEnvironment env)

{

if (env.IsDevelopment())

{

app.UseDeveloperExceptionPage();
```

```
}

else

{

app.UseExceptionHandler("/Home/Error");

app.UseHsts();

}

app.UseHttpsRedirection();

app.UseStaticFiles();

app.UseRouting();

app.UseAuthorization();

app.UseEndpoints(endpoints =>

{

endpoints.MapControllerRoute(

name: "default",

pattern: "{controller=Home}/{action=Index}/{id?}");

});

}
```

How the Startup Class Works

- **Initialization**: The Startup class is initialized when the application starts. ASP.NET Core uses conventions to find and use this class.

- **Service Configuration**: The ConfigureServices method is called first to set up the services needed by the application.

- **Middleware Configuration**: The Configure method is called next to set up the middleware pipeline that processes incoming

HTTP requests.

Benefits of the Startup Class

- **Centralized Configuration**: All service and middleware configurations are centralized in one place.

- **Modularity**: Services and middleware can be easily added, removed, or modified.

- **Flexibility**: The application can be configured differently for development, staging, and production environments.

Example of startup class in ASP.NET Core.

Here's an example of a Startup class in an ASP.NET Core application. This example demonstrates how to configure services and middleware for a simple web application:

Example of a Startup Class

```
public class Startup

{

public Startup(IConfiguration configuration)

{

Configuration = configuration;

}

public IConfiguration Configuration { get; }

// This method gets called by the runtime. Use this method to add services to the container.

public void ConfigureServices(IServiceCollection services)

{

// Add framework services.
```

```csharp
services.AddControllersWithViews();

// Add a database context (e.g., Entity Framework Core)

services.AddDbContext<MyDbContext>(options =>

options.UseSqlServer(Configuration.GetConnectionString("DefaultC
onnection")));

// Add a custom service

services.AddTransient<IMyService, MyService>();

}

// This method gets called by the runtime. Use this method to configure
the HTTP request pipeline.

public void Configure(IApplicationBuilder app, IWebHostEnviron-
ment env)

{

if (env.IsDevelopment())

{

app.UseDeveloperExceptionPage();

}

else

{

app.UseExceptionHandler("/Home/Error");

app.UseHsts();

}

app.UseHttpsRedirection();

app.UseStaticFiles();
```

app.UseRouting();

app.UseAuthorization();

app.UseEndpoints(endpoints =>

{

endpoints.MapControllerRoute(

name: "default",

pattern: "{controller=Home}/{action=Index}/{id?}");

});

}

}

Breakdown of the Example

1. **Constructor**:

   - The Startup class constructor receives an IConfiguration object, which is used to access configuration settings.

2. **ConfigureServices Method**:

   - **AddControllersWithViews**: Adds support for controllers and views (MVC).

   - **AddDbContext**: Registers a database context with Entity Framework Core, using a connection string from the configuration.

   - **AddTransient**: Registers a custom service with a transient lifetime.

3. **Configure Method**:

   - **Environment Check**: Configures error handling based on the environment (development or production).

- ○ **Middleware**:

  - UseHttpsRedirection: Redirects HTTP requests to HTTPS.

  - UseStaticFiles: Serves static files like HTML, CSS, and JavaScript.

  - UseRouting: Adds routing middleware to the request pipeline.

  - UseAuthorization: Adds authorization middleware.

  - UseEndpoints: Configures endpoint routing for controllers.

This example sets up a basic ASP.NET Core application with MVC support, a database context, and a custom service. You can customize the Startup class further based on your application's requirements.

What are the different service lifetimes in .NET Core?

In .NET Core, service lifetimes determine how long instances of services are maintained by the dependency injection (DI) container. There are three primary service lifetimes:

1. Transient

- **Description**: Transient services are created each time they are requested. This means a new instance is provided every time a service is injected or requested.

- **Use Case**: Ideal for lightweight, stateless services that do not maintain any state between method calls.

Example:services.AddTransient<IMyService, MyService>();

2. Scoped

- **Description**: Scoped services are created once per request. A single instance is used throughout the lifespan of a request.

- **Use Case**: Suitable for services that need to maintain state within a single request, such as database contexts in web applications.

Example:services.AddScoped<IMyService, MyService>();

3. Singleton

- **Description**: Singleton services are created once and shared across the entire application. The same instance is used for every request and throughout the application's lifetime.

- **Use Case**: Best for services that maintain state or hold expensive resources that need to be shared across the application.

Example:services.AddSingleton<IMyService, MyService>();

Summary of Service Lifetimes

- **Transient**: New instance per request.

- **Scoped**: One instance per request.

- **Singleton**: One instance for the entire application.

How do you handle configuration in ASP.NET Core?

Handling configuration in ASP.NET Core is flexible and powerful, allowing you to manage settings from various sources such as JSON files, environment variables, command-line arguments, and more. Here's a comprehensive guide on how to handle configuration in ASP.NET Core:

Configuration Sources

1. **Appsettings.json**: The most common way to store configuration settings. Supports hierarchical data.

```
{

"Logging": {

"LogLevel": {
```

"Default": "Information",

"Microsoft": "Warning"

}

},

"ConnectionStrings": {

"DefaultConnection":   "Server=myServer;Database=myDB;User Id=myUser;Password=myPass;"

}

}

1. **Environment Variables**: Useful for overriding settings in different environments (e.g., development, production).

```
export ConnectionStrings__DefaultConnection="Server=myProdServer;Database=myProdDB;User              Id=myProdUser;Password=myProdPass;"
```

1. **Command-Line Arguments**: Can be used to pass configuration settings when starting the application.

```
dotnet    run    --ConnectionStrings:DefaultConnection="Server=myCmdServer;Database=myCmdDB;User Id=myCmdUser;Password=myCmdPass;"
```

1. **User Secrets**: Ideal for storing sensitive information during development.

```
dotnet    user-secrets    set    "ConnectionStrings:DefaultConnection" "Server=mySecretServer;Database=mySecretDB;User Id=mySecretUser;Password=mySecretPass;"
```

Accessing Configuration

1. **Using IConfiguration**:

   - Inject IConfiguration into your classes to access configuration settings.

```
public class MyService

{

private readonly IConfiguration _configuration;

public MyService(IConfiguration configuration)

{

_configuration = configuration;

}

public void PrintConnectionString()

{

var connectionString = _configuration.GetConnectionString("Defaul
tConnection");

Console.WriteLine(connectionString);

}

}
```

1. **Binding Configuration to Strongly Typed Objects**:

   ◦ Bind configuration sections to POCO classes for easier ac-
     cess.

```
public class MySettings

{

public string DefaultConnection { get; set; }

}

public void ConfigureServices(IServiceCollection services)

{
```

```
services.Configure<MySettings>(Configuration.GetSection("Connecti
onStrings"));

}

public class MyService

{

private readonly MySettings _settings;

public MyService(IOptions<MySettings> settings)

{

_settings = settings.Value;

}

public void PrintConnectionString()

{

Console.WriteLine(_settings.DefaultConnection);

}

}
```

Setting Up Configuration in Program.cs

In ASP.NET Core 6.0 and later, configuration is typically set up in the Program.cs file:

```
var builder = WebApplication.CreateBuilder(args);

// Add services to the container.

builder.Services.AddControllersWithViews();

// Add configuration sources

builder.Configuration

.AddJsonFile("appsettings.json", optional: false, reloadOnChange: true)
```

.AddJsonFile($"appsettings.{builder.Environment.Environment-Name}.json", optional: true)

.AddEnvironmentVariables()

.AddCommandLine(args);

var app = builder.Build();

// Configure the HTTP request pipeline.

if (!app.Environment.IsDevelopment())

{

app.UseExceptionHandler("/Home/Error");

app.UseHsts();

}

app.UseHttpsRedirection();

app.UseStaticFiles();

app.UseRouting();

app.UseAuthorization();

app.MapControllerRoute(

name: "default",

pattern: "{controller=Home}/{action=Index}/{id?}");

app.Run();

Summary

- **Flexible Sources**: Configuration can come from JSON files, environment variables, command-line arguments, and more.

- **IConfiguration Interface**: Access configuration settings using the IConfiguration interface.

- **Strongly Typed Options**: Bind configuration sections to strongly typed classes for easier management.

Explain the concept of routing in ASP.NET Core.

Routing in ASP.NET Core is the process of mapping incoming HTTP requests to the appropriate controller actions or endpoints. It plays a crucial role in directing requests to the correct part of your application based on the URL and HTTP method.

Key Concepts of Routing

1. **Route Templates**:

   ○ Define patterns for URLs that the application can handle.

   ○ Can include parameters to capture values from the URL.

app.MapControllerRoute(

name: "default",

pattern: "{controller=Home}/{action=Index}/{id?}");

1. **Conventional Routing**:

   ○ Uses predefined patterns to match URLs to controller actions.

   ○ Typically defined in the Startup class or Program.cs.

app.UseEndpoints(endpoints =>

{

endpoints.MapControllerRoute(

name: "default",

pattern: "{controller=Home}/{action=Index}/{id?}");

});

1. **Attribute Routing**:

   - Uses attributes to define routes directly on controller actions.

   - Provides more control and flexibility over route definitions.

[Route("api/[controller]")]

public class ProductsController : Controller

{

[HttpGet("{id}")]

public IActionResult GetProduct(int id)

{

// Action code

}

}

1. **Endpoint Routing**:

   - Introduced in ASP.NET Core 3.0, it unifies routing for MVC, Razor Pages, SignalR, and more.

   - Configured using UseRouting and UseEndpoints middleware.

app.UseRouting();

app.UseEndpoints(endpoints =>

{

endpoints.MapControllers();

endpoints.MapRazorPages();

});

Example of Routing in ASP.NET Core

Here's a simple example to illustrate routing in an ASP.NET Core application:

Define Routes in Program.cs:var builder = WebApplication.CreateBuilder(args);

var app = builder.Build();

app.UseRouting();

app.UseEndpoints(endpoints =>

{

endpoints.MapControllerRoute(

name: "default",

pattern: "{controller=Home}/{action=Index}/{id?}");

});

app.Run();

Controller with Attribute Routing:[Route("api/[controller]")]

public class ProductsController : Controller

{

[HttpGet("{id}")]

public IActionResult GetProduct(int id)

{

// Retrieve and return the product

return Ok(new { Id = id, Name = "Sample Product" });

}

}

Benefits of Routing

- **URL Mapping**: Easily map URLs to specific actions or endpoints.

- **Flexibility**: Use conventional or attribute routing based on your needs.

- **Maintainability**: Centralized route definitions make it easier to manage and update routes.

Explain the difference between appsettings.json and appsettings.{Environment}.json.

In ASP.NET Core, the appsettings.json and appsettings.{Environment}.json files, such as appsettings.Development.json, are used to manage configuration settings for different environments. Here's a breakdown of their differences and purposes:

appsettings.json

- **Purpose**: Serves as the base configuration file for the application.

- **Content**: Contains settings that are common across all environments.

- **Usage**: This file is always loaded, regardless of the environment.

appsettings.{Environment}.json

- **Purpose**: Provides environment-specific configuration settings.

- **Content**: Contains settings that override those in appsettings.json for a specific environment (e.g., Development, Production, Staging).

- **Usage**: Loaded based on the current environment. For example, appsettings.Development.json is loaded when the application is running in the Development environment.

How They Work Together?

When the application starts, ASP.NET Core loads configuration settings in a specific order. The settings in appsettings.{Environment}.json files override those in appsettings.json if there are any conflicts. This allows you to have a base configuration and then customize it for different environments.

Example

appsettings.json:

{

"Logging": {

"LogLevel": {

"Default": "Information",

"Microsoft": "Warning"

}

},

"ConnectionStrings": {

"DefaultConnection": "Server=prodServer;Database=prodDB;User Id=prodUser;Password=prodPass;"

}

}

appsettings.Development.json:

{

"Logging": {

"LogLevel": {

"Default": "Debug",

"Microsoft": "Information"

}

},

"ConnectionStrings": {

"DefaultConnection":   "Server=devServer;Database=devDB;User Id=devUser;Password=devPass;"

}

}

In this example:

- The Logging settings in appsettings.Development.json will override those in appsettings.json when the application is running in the Development environment.

- The ConnectionStrings setting in appsettings.Development.json will also override the one in appsettings.json.

Benefits

- **Flexibility**: Easily manage different configurations for different environments without changing the base configuration file.

- **Maintainability**: Keep environment-specific settings separate, making it easier to manage and update configurations.

How do you secure an ASP.NET Core application?

Securing an ASP.NET Core application involves a layered approach, addressing different aspects of the application's interaction with users and data. Here's a breakdown of key areas to focus on:

Authentication and Authorization:

Strong User Authentication:

- Implement ASP.NET Core Identity for user registration, login, and management.

- Enforce strong password policies with minimum length, complexity requirements, and lockout mechanisms for failed login attempts.

- Consider integrating two-factor authentication (2FA) for an extra layer of security.

Authorization:

- Use role-based access control (RBAC) to define permissions for different user roles.

- Implement authorization policies to restrict access to specific functionalities based on user roles or claims.

Data Protection:

Input Validation:

- Validate all user input to prevent attacks like Cross-Site Scripting (XSS) and SQL injection.

- Use built-in ASP.NET Core model validation or third-party libraries for comprehensive validation.

- Sanitize user input before using it in queries or storing it in the database.

Secure Data Storage:

- Never store sensitive information like passwords in plain text.

- Use hashing and salting techniques to securely store passwords.

- Consider using a dedicated data protection library for encrypting sensitive data at rest and in transit.

Secure Communication:

HTTPS Enforcement:

- Enforce HTTPS communication to encrypt all traffic between the client and server.

- Configure your application to redirect all HTTP requests to HTTPS automatically.

CSRF/XSRF (Cross-Site Request Forgery) Prevention:

- Implement anti-CSRF tokens to prevent unauthorized actions on behalf of a logged-in user.

- Use built-in ASP.NET Core features or third-party libraries for CSRF protection.

Additional Considerations:

Error Handling:

- Implement custom error pages to avoid revealing sensitive information about your application in case of errors.

- Log and monitor errors for troubleshooting and security analysis.

Secret Management:

- Never store application secrets (like connection strings) directly in your code.

- Use environment variables or a dedicated secret management service to store and access secrets securely.

Regular Updates:

- Keep your application and its dependencies updated to address known vulnerabilities.

- Regularly scan your application for security weaknesses using security scanners.

What is Transfer-encoding?

Transfer-encoding in .NET Core is a mechanism used to specify how the message body of an HTTP request or response should be interpreted by the receiver. It provides flexibility in how content is transmitted, especially when dealing with large or unknown-sized data.

Key Points:

- **Chunked Encoding:** This is the most common transfer encoding used in .NET Core. It allows for the transmission of unknown-sized content by dividing it into chunks, each preceded by its length in hexadecimal.

- **Compression:** .NET Core supports compression using the deflate and gzip algorithms. This can significantly reduce the size of the message body, leading to faster transmission and reduced network usage.

- **Custom Transfer-encoding:** While less common, you can create custom transfer encodings if needed. However, it's generally recommended to use standard transfer encodings for compatibility.

How to Use Transfer-encoding in .NET Core:

Set the TransferEncoding Property: When sending a response from your ASP.NET Core application, set the TransferEncoding property of the HttpResponse object to the desired transfer encoding. For exampl e:response.TransferEncoding = TransferEncoding.Chunked;

Write the Content: Write the content of the message body to the response stream. If you're using chunked encoding, write the content in chunks.

Example:

using Microsoft.AspNetCore.Mvc;

namespace YourNamespace

{

```
public class HomeController : Controller

{

public IActionResult Index()

{

var response = Response;

response.TransferEncoding = TransferEncoding.Chunked;

using (var writer = response.BodyWriter)

{

for (int i = 0; i < 10; i++)

{

var chunk = Encoding.UTF8.GetBytes($"Chunk {i}\r\n");

writer.Write(chunk);

writer.Write(chunk.Length.ToString("x"));

writer.Write("\r\n");

}

writer.Write("0\r\n\r\n"); // End of chunked encoding

}

return new EmptyResult();

}

}
}
```

Important Considerations:

- **Compatibility:** Ensure that the client receiving the response supports the specified transfer encoding.

- **Performance:** Consider the trade-offs between compression and decompression overhead. In some cases, compression may not be beneficial if the original content is already small.

- **Custom Encodings:** If you create custom transfer encodings, be aware of potential compatibility issues and security risks.

Difference between app.Run and app.Use in middleware configuration.

Both app.Run and app.Use are used in middleware configuration for ASP.NET Core applications, but they serve distinct purposes:

1. app.Run:

- **Purpose:** Marks the **end** of the request pipeline. It defines the **terminal middleware**.

- **Behavior:**

  - Any middleware configured **after** app.Run will **not** be executed for the request.

  - The middleware defined in app.Run handles the request and returns the response.

- **Use Case:**

  - You want a specific middleware to handle all incoming requests and generate the final response.

  - This is often used for simple static content serving or basic error handling.

2. app.Use:

Purpose: Adds a middleware component to the **request processing pipeline**.

Behavior:

- Each middleware defined with app.Use gets invoked sequentially in the order they are configured.

- The middleware can:

    ○ Access the request context (HttpContext).

    ○ Modify the request or response.

    ○ Optionally call the **next** middleware in the pipeline using await next.InvokeAsync(context).

- Middleware can be used for various tasks like authentication, authorization, routing, logging, etc.

Key Differences:

Example:

public void Configure(IApplicationBuilder app, IWebHostEnvironment env)

{

if (env.IsDevelopment())

{

app.UseDeveloperExceptionPage();

}

// This middleware

would be the terminal one

app.Run(async context =>

{

context.Response.Headers.Add("Content-Type", "text/plain");

await context.Response.WriteAsync("Hello from the terminal middleware!");

```
});

// These middlewares would not be executed because app.Run is above
them

// app.UseRouting();

// app.UseEndpoints(endpoints =>

// {

//    endpoints.MapControllers();

// });

}
```

What is a Request delegate and how is it used?

A request delegate in ASP.NET Core is a function that handles incoming HTTP requests. It represents a piece of middleware that can process a request and potentially modify the response before passing it on to the next middleware in the pipeline.

Key characteristics of a request delegate:

- **Signature:** A request delegate has a specific signature: Func<HttpContext, Task>.

- **HttpContext:** The HttpContext object provides information about the incoming request and outgoing response, including headers, cookies, body, and more.

- **Task:** The request delegate returns a Task object, which represents an asynchronous operation. This allows for non-blocking operations and efficient handling of concurrent requests.

How request delegates are used:

- **Middleware:** Request delegates are the building blocks of middleware components. Middleware can perform various tasks such as authentication, authorization, routing, logging, and more.

- **Endpoint Routing:** In .NET Core, endpoint routing uses request delegates to match incoming requests to specific endpoints (e.g., controllers and actions).

- **Custom Middleware:** You can create custom middleware by defining your own request delegate and adding it to the middleware pipeline using app.Use.

- **Terminal Middleware:** The final middleware in the pipeline is typically a request delegate that handles the final response and sends it back to the client.

Example:

app.Use(async (context, next) =>

{

// Perform some logic before the request is processed

await next.Invoke(context);

// Perform some logic after the request is processed

});

Describe the Host in ASP.NET Core.

The **Host** is a fundamental concept in ASP.NET Core applications. It acts as the **entry point** for the application, responsible for its **startup and lifetime management**. Here's a breakdown of its key functions:

Responsibilities of the Host:

- **Configuration:** The Host reads configuration settings from various sources like environment variables, appsettings.json files, and command-line arguments.

- **Dependency Injection:** The Host creates and manages the dependency injection container that provides services to your application components.

- **Middleware Pipeline:** The Host sets up the middleware

pipeline, which is a sequence of components that handle incoming HTTP requests.

- **Server Configuration:** The Host can configure the underlying web server (like Kestrel) to listen on specific ports and handle different protocols (HTTP/1.1, HTTP/2).

- **Application Lifetime:** The Host manages the lifecycle of your application, including startup, shutdown, and handling events like application termination signals.

Types of Hosts in ASP.NET Core:

- **Web Host (Legacy):** This is the traditional host used in earlier versions of ASP.NET Core. It's focused on web applications and provides direct integration with Kestrel as the web server. While still supported for backward compatibility, the Generic Host is generally recommended for new applications.

- **Generic Host:** This is the recommended host for most new ASP.NET Core applications. It's more versatile, allowing you to host not just web applications but also background services, console applications, and more. The Generic Host can be configured to work with different web servers or serverless environments.

Benefits of using the Host:

- **Centralized Startup Logic:** The Host provides a clear separation of concerns, keeping startup and configuration logic centralized in one place.

- **Extensibility:** The Host allows you to customize its behavior through configuration options and extensions.

- **Testability:** The Host abstraction makes it easier to test your application components in isolation.

Explain Session and State Management in ASP.NET Core.

In ASP.NET Core, maintaining state across user requests is important for applications that require users to be logged in, track shopping carts, or store temporary information. Here's an overview of Session and other state management options:

1. Session State:

- **Purpose:** Session state allows you to store user-specific data on the server during a user's browsing session.

- **How it works:**

    - A unique session ID is generated for each user and stored in a cookie on the client-side.

    - The server stores the session data associated with the session ID.

    - Subsequent requests from the same user include the session ID, allowing the server to retrieve the associated data.

- **Benefits:**

    - Simple to use and understand.

    - Suitable for storing user-specific data during a session.

- **Drawbacks:**

    - Relies on cookies, which can be disabled by users.

    - Session data is lost when the session expires or the browser is closed.

    - Not ideal for applications requiring high scalability or data persistence across restarts.

2. TempData:

- **Purpose:** TempData is a mechanism for storing temporary data that persists only for the next request.

- **How it works:**

  - TempData is stored in the user's session state but is automatically cleared after being accessed in a subsequent request.

- **Benefits:**

  - Useful for passing data from one controller action to another within a single request lifecycle.

  - Eliminates the need for complex session management in simple scenarios.

- **Drawbacks:**

  - Data is lost after the next request, not suitable for longer-term storage.

  - Relies on session state, inheriting its limitations.

3. Cookies:

- **Purpose:** Cookies are small pieces of data stored on the client-side (user's browser).

- **How it works:**

  - The server sends cookie data to the browser, which stores it for a defined period.

  - Subsequent requests from the same browser include the cookies in the request header.

  - You can store various data in cookies, including user preferences or authentication tokens.

- **Benefits:**

  - Persistent storage across multiple sessions if expiration time allows.

- Can be used for client-side state management.

- **Drawbacks:**

  - Limited storage size (4KB per cookie).

  - Users can disable cookies or delete them manually.

  - Security concerns if sensitive data is stored.

4. Client-side Storage:

- **Purpose:** Client-side storage options like Local Storage and Session Storage allow you to store data directly in the user's browser.

- **How it works:**

  - Data is stored using JavaScript APIs in the browser's local storage or session storage.

  - This data is accessible within the same browser window or tab.

- **Benefits:**

  - No server-side dependency for data storage and retrieval.

  - Faster access compared to server-side storage.

- **Drawbacks:**

  - Limited storage size and functionality compared to server-side options.

  - Data is accessible only from the same browser window or tab.

  - Security concerns as data is not encrypted and accessible to client-side scripts.

5. Database:

- **Purpose:** Databases are the most robust and scalable option for storing persistent application state.

- **How it works:**

  - Application data is stored in a database management system like SQL Server or MongoDB.

  - Your application uses database access libraries to interact with the data.

- **Benefits:**

  - Persistent storage even across application restarts and server sessions.

  - Scalability for handling large amounts of data.

  - Security can be managed through database access controls.

- **Drawbacks:**

  - More complex setup and maintenance compared to other options.

  - Requires additional infrastructure and expertise in managing databases.

Choosing the right option depends on your specific needs:

- **Simple user data during a session:** Session State or TempData.

- **Temporary data for a single request:** TempData.

- **Persistent user preferences:** Cookies.

- **Client-side state management within a single window/tab:** Client-side Storage.

- **Large amounts of persistent data requiring security:**

Database.

Describe Model Binding in ASP.NET Core. Explain Custom Model Binding.

Model binding is a powerful feature in ASP.NET Core that simplifies the process of mapping data from incoming HTTP requests to objects in your application. It bridges the gap between the raw HTTP request data and your strongly typed models, allowing you to focus on business logic instead of manual data parsing.

Here's how it works:

1. **Request Data Sources:** Model binding can access data from various sources in an HTTP request:

   - **Route data:** Values from URL segments captured by routing.

   - **Query string parameters:** Key-value pairs appended to the URL after the question mark.

   - **Form data:** Data submitted through HTML forms.

   - **Request body:** Data sent in the request body, typically in JSON or XML format for APIs.

   - **Headers:** Specific headers in the request.

2. **Matching:** Model binding attempts to match the incoming data with the properties of your model class. This matching is typically based on property names by default.

3. **Conversion:** If necessary, model binding attempts to convert the data from its string representation (e.g., from a form input) to the appropriate type of the model property. It uses built-in type converters or TryParse methods to achieve this.

4. **Validation:** Once the data is mapped, model binding can optionally perform validation on the model properties using data annotations or custom validation logic.

5. **Populating the Model:** If everything is successful, the model binding system populates an instance of your model class with the mapped and validated data. This model instance is then passed as an argument to your controller action methods or other parts of your application.

Benefits of Model Binding:

- **Reduced code:** Eliminates the need for manual parsing and conversion of request data.

- **Improved maintainability:** Separates data access logic from your business logic.

- **Strong typing:** Ensures data type safety and avoids potential conversion errors.

- **Flexibility:** Supports various data sources and complex model structures.

Custom Model Binding

While model binding provides great out-of-the-box functionality, there might be situations where you need more control over binding logic. This is where **custom model binding** comes into play.

Here's when you might need custom model binding:

- **Complex Data Structures:** When your model requires custom parsing logic beyond simple type conversion.

- **Specific Data Sources:** To handle data from non-standard sources not directly supported by default model binding.

- **Advanced Validation:** When you require more sophisticated validation rules not covered by data annotations.

Creating a Custom Model Binder:

1. **Implement the IModelBinder interface:** This interface defines methods for binding a request to a model instance.

2. **Provide Binding Logic:** Implement the BindModelAsync

method to define how data from the request should be extracted and converted to your model object.

3. **Register the Binder:** Use the [ModelBinder(typeof(YourCustomModelBinder))] attribute to associate the custom binder with your model class.

Example:

```
public class PriceModelBinder : IModelBinder

{

public async Task BindModelAsync(ActionContext actionContext,
ModelBindingContext bindingContext)

{

if (bindingContext.ModelType == typeof(Price))

{

var valueProvider = bindingContext.ValueProvider;

var valueFromQuery = valueProvider.GetValue("price");

if (valueFromQuery.TryGetValue(out var valueString))

{

decimal price;

if (decimal.TryParse(valueString.Replace("$", ""), out price))

{

bindingContext.Result = Success(new Price { Value = price });

}

else

{

bindingContext.ModelState.AddModelError(
```

```
bindingContext.ModelName,

"Invalid price format."

);

}

}

}

}

}

public class Price

{

public decimal Value { get; set; }

}

public class MyController

{

[HttpGet]

public IActionResult GetProductPrice([ModelBinder(typeof(Price-
ModelBinder))] Price price)

{

// Use the bound price object

}

}
```

Explain Model Validation and how to perform custom validation.

Model validation is a critical aspect of building robust web applications. It ensures that incoming data adheres to predefined rules and constraints, preventing invalid data from entering your system. ASP.NET Core provides built-in mechanisms for model validation, as well as the flexibility to implement custom validation logic.

Built-in Validation:

ASP.NET Core offers a variety of built-in validation attributes that can be applied to model properties to enforce common validation rules:

- **Required:** Ensures that a property is not null or empty.

- **StringLength:** Validates the length of a string.

- **Range:** Checks if a numeric value falls within a specified range.

- **RegularExpression:** Validates a string against a regular expression pattern.

- **EmailAddress:** Verifies if a string is a valid email address.

- **Compare:** Compares two properties for equality or inequality.

Example:

```
public class Product

{

[Required]

public string Name { get; set; }

[Range(0.01, double.MaxValue)]

public decimal Price { get; set; }

[RegularExpression(@"^\d{4}-\d{2}-\d{2}$")]
```

```
public string ReleaseDate { get; set; }

}
```

Custom Validation:

When built-in attributes don't suffice, you can create custom validation logic using the following approaches:

1. Data Annotations:

- Create a custom validation attribute that inherits from ValidationAttribute.

- Override the IsValid method to implement your custom validation logic.

- Apply the attribute to your model property.

Example:

```
public class PositivePriceAttribute : ValidationAttribute

{

public override bool IsValid(object value)

{

if (value is decimal price && price > 0)

{

return true;

}

return false;

}

}
```

2. Model Validation Context:

- Use the ValidationContext object to access additional information about the validation process.

- Implement custom validation logic within your model class or a separate validation service.

Example:

public class Product

{

[ValidateProperty(ErrorMessage = "Price must be positive.")]

public decimal Price { get; set; }

public bool IsValid(ValidationContext validationContext)

{

if (Price <= 0)

{

validationContext.AddValidationResult(new ValidationResult("Price must be positive.", new[] { nameof(Price) }));

return false;

}

return true;

}

}

3. Model Binder:

- Create a custom model binder and override its BindModelAsync method.

- Implement validation logic within the model binder and set the ModelState accordingly.

Example:

```csharp
public class PositivePriceModelBinder : IModelBinder

{

public async Task BindModelAsync(ActionContext actionContext,
ModelBindingContext bindingContext)

{

if (bindingContext.ModelType == typeof(decimal))

{

var value = bindingContext.ValueProvider.GetValue("Price").FirstValu
e;

if (decimal.TryParse(value, out var price) && price > 0)

{

bindingContext.Result = ModelBindingResult.Success(price);

}

else

{

bindingContext.ModelState.AddModelError(bindingContext.Model
Name, "Price must be positive.");

}

}

}
```

Model Validation in Action:

ASP.NET Core automatically validates models before calling controller actions. If validation fails, the model state becomes invalid, and the controller action is not executed.

You can use the ModelState.IsValid property to check if the model is valid and return appropriate responses (e.g., bad request, validation errors) based on the validation results.

What is the Options Pattern and how is it used in ASP.NET Core configuration?

The Options pattern is a design pattern in ASP.NET Core used for managing application configuration settings in a structured and efficient way. It provides a mechanism to define strongly typed classes to represent groups of related configuration settings and simplifies access to those settings throughout your application.

Here's how the Options pattern works:

1. **Define Options Class:** You create a class that represents a group of configuration settings. This class typically has public properties that map to the corresponding configuration keys.

2. **Bind Configuration:** You use dependency injection to inject an instance of IOptions<TOptions> where TOptions is your configuration class. This injects an object that holds the populated configuration values based on your class definition.

Benefits of the Options Pattern:

Strongly-typed access: Ensures type safety and prevents errors that might occur with string-based configuration access.

Improved readability: Makes configuration settings easier to understand and manage within your code.

Centralized configuration: Groups related settings together for better organization.

Validation: Allows for optional configuration validation to ensure settings are within expected ranges or formats.

Default values: Provides a way to define default values for configuration settings if not explicitly defined in configuration sources.

Using the Options Pattern:

1. **Configure Services:** In your Startup.cs file, configure your services to bind the configuration to your options class using the Configure method:

services.Configure<MyOptions>(configuration.GetSection("MyOptio ns"));

1. **Inject Options:** Inject the IOptions<MyOptions> instance in your controllers, services, or other parts of your application using dependency injection:

public class MyController

{

private readonly IOptions<MyOptions> _options;

public MyController(IOptions<MyOptions> options)

{

_options = options;

}

public IActionResult MyAction()

{

var apiKey = _options.Value.ApiKey;

// Use the configuration values

}

}

Advanced Features:

Validation: You can implement custom validation logic within your options class to ensure configuration settings meet specific criteria.

Multiple Configuration Sources: The options pattern supports multiple configuration sources, allowing you to load settings from different files or environments.

Snapshots vs. Singletons: You can choose between IOptions<TOptions> which provides a singleton instance of configuration or IOptionsSnapshot<TOptions> which provides a snapshot at the time of injection, allowing for configuration changes to be reflected.

How to configure and manage multiple environments in ASP.NET Core applications?

Below are the ways to configure and manage multiple environments in ASP.NET Core applications:

1. Environment Variables:

- **ASPNETCORE_ENVIRONMENT:** This environment variable is used by ASP.NET Core to determine the current runtime environment. You can set it in your development machine's environment variables, cloud platform settings, or container configurations.

- **Custom Environment Variables:** Define additional environment variables specific to each environment (e.g., DevelopmentConnectionString, StagingConnectionString, ProductionConnectionString). Set these variables based on your deployment environment.

2. Configuration Files:

- **appsettings.json:** This serves as the base configuration file for all environments. It can contain common settings applicable across environments.

- **appsettings.{Environment}.json:** Create separate JSON files for each environment (e.g., appsettings.Development.json , appsettings.Staging.json, appsettings.Production.json). These

files can override or supplement settings from the base appset
tings.json.

Using Configuration in Code:

- Inject IConfiguration into your Startup.cs file or other parts of
  your application.

- Use the Configuration object to access settings based on the
  environment variable value:

```
var connectionString = configuration.GetConnectionString("Default
Connection");

if (Environment.GetEnvironmentVariable("ASPNETCORE_ENVI
RONMENT") == "Development")

{

// Use development-specific configuration

}

else if (Environment.GetEnvironmentVariable("ASPNETCORE_EN
VIRONMENT") == "Staging")

{

// Use staging-specific configuration

}

else

{

// Use production-specific configuration

}
```

3. Conditional Configuration with IHostingEnvironment:

- Inject IHostingEnvironment into your Startup.cs file.

- Use properties like IsDevelopment, IsStaging, or IsProduction to conditionally configure based on the environment:

```
if (hostingEnvironment.IsDevelopment())

{

// Use development-specific configuration

}

else if (hostingEnvironment.IsStaging())

{

// Use staging-specific configuration

}

else

{

// Use production-specific configuration

}
```

4. Using a Configuration Provider: Create a custom configuration provider to read environment-specific settings from specific locations (e.g., database, key vault) and integrate it with the overall configuration system.

Benefits of using Multiple Environments:

- **Isolation:** Develop and test features in a separate environment (staging) before deploying to production.

- **Configuration Isolation:** Use environment-specific settings for databases, logging, and other aspects of your application.

- **Improved Configurability:** Manage configurations more effectively without hardcoding sensitive information into the application.

Choosing the Right Approach:

- For simple scenarios, environment variables and separate configuration files might suffice.

- For complex configuration needs, consider custom configuration providers or frameworks like ConfigurationBuilder for advanced management.

How to access the HttpContext object within an ASP .NET Core application?

The HttpContext object is a fundamental element in ASP.NET Core applications. It provides access to information about the current HTTP request and response, allowing you to perform various tasks like:

- **Accessing request details:** Headers, cookies, query strings, route data, and the request body.

- **Generating responses:** Setting status codes, headers, and sending content back to the client.

- **Managing sessions:** Storing and retrieving session data associated with the user.

- **Authentication and authorization:** Identifying the logged-in user and checking access permissions.

- **Dependency injection:** Accessing services registered in the dependency injection container within the context of the request.

There are two primary ways to access the HttpContext object in your ASP.NET Core application:

1. Accessing HttpContext in Controllers:

By default, ASP.NET Core automatically injects the HttpContext object as a parameter into your controller action methods. You can then use its properties and methods to access request and response information:

public class HomeController : Controller

```
{

public IActionResult Index(HttpContext context)

{

// Access request headers

var userAgent = context.Request.Headers["User-Agent"];

// Set response status code

context.Response.StatusCode = 201;

// Write content to the response

await context.Response.WriteAsync("Hello from ASP.NET Core!");

return View();

}

}
```

2. Accessing HttpContext using IHttpContextAccessor:

In some scenarios, you might need to access the HttpContext outside of controller actions, such as within services or custom middleware. For this purpose, ASP.NET Core provides the IHttpContextAccessor interface:

```
public class MyService

{

private readonly IHttpContextAccessor _httpContextAccessor;

public MyService(IHttpContextAccessor

httpContextAccessor)

{

_httpContextAccessor = httpContextAccessor;

}
```

```
public string GetCurrentUserId()

{

if (_httpContextAccessor.HttpContext?.User?.Identity?.IsAuthentic
ated == true)

{

return _httpContextAccessor.HttpContext.User.Identity.Name;

}

return null;

}

}
```

However, using IHttpContextAccessor should be considered a secondary option. It's generally recommended to keep your application logic decoupled from the context and inject necessary dependencies like user identity through the constructor whenever possible. This promotes better testability and separation of concerns.

What is a Change Token in ASP.NET Core Development?

In ASP.NET Core, a **Change Token** is a lightweight mechanism for notifying your code when a specific resource or data has been modified. It allows you to implement efficient caching and reactive programming patterns within your applications.

Key characteristics of Change Tokens:

- **Represents Mutability:** A Change Token indicates that the associated resource or data is potentially subject to change.

- **Asynchronous Notification:** Change Tokens provide an asynchronous notification mechanism, allowing your code to react to changes without blocking threads.

- **Cancelable:** Change Tokens can be canceled, indicating that your code is no longer interested in receiving change notifications for that specific resource.

How Change Tokens are used:

- **File Monitoring:** The IFileProvider interface in ASP.NET Core provides methods like Watch that return a Change Token. This token can be used to detect modifications to specific files or folders, triggering cache invalidation or other actions when a change occurs.

- **Configuration Changes:** The IOptionsMonitor interface used for managing application configuration settings in ASP.NET Core provides an overload that accepts IOptionsChangeTokenSource instances. This allows you to register for notifications when the configuration settings are updated, potentially refreshing cached configuration values.

- **Custom Implementations:** You can create your own custom implementations of Change Tokens to notify interested parties when any data or resource within your application changes.

Benefits of using Change Tokens:

- **Improved Performance:** Change Tokens enable efficient caching by invalidating cached data only when changes occur, avoiding unnecessary recalculations.

- **Reactive Programming:** Change Tokens are compatible with reactive programming patterns, allowing your application to react dynamically to changes in its state or environment.

- **Decoupled Monitoring:** The code using the Change Token is decoupled from the source of change, promoting modularity and cleaner code.

Example with File Monitoring:

```
var fileProvider = application.Services.GetRequiredService<IFileProvi
der>();
```

```
var changeToken = fileProvider.Watch("data.json");
```

changeToken.RegisterChangeCallback(async (state) =>

{

// Invalidate cache or perform other actions based on file change

}, null);

Describe the URL Rewriting Middleware in ASP.NET Core and its applications.

In ASP.NET Core, URL Rewriting Middleware is a powerful tool that allows you to manipulate incoming URLs before they reach your application logic. It provides a way to modify the URL structure for various purposes, enhancing user experience and maintaining compatibility with older URLs.

Key functionalities of URL Rewriting Middleware:

- **Redirecting Requests:** You can redirect requests from one URL to another, permanently (using HTTP status code 301) or temporarily (using code 302). This can be useful for handling legacy URLs, moving resources, or implementing vanity URLs.

- **Rewriting Paths:** The middleware can rewrite portions of the URL path. This allows you to create a cleaner and more consistent URL structure for your application.

- **Query String Manipulation:** You can modify or add query string parameters based on rewrite rules.

Benefits of using URL Rewriting Middleware:

- **Clean URLs:** Rewrites can improve the aesthetics and user-friendliness of your application's URLs.

- **Legacy URL Support:** Maintain compatibility with older URLs by directing them to the appropriate resources within your application.

- **SEO Optimization:** Well-structured URLs can be beneficial for search engine optimization.

- **Load Balancing:** You can rewrite URLs to distribute requests across multiple servers in a load balancing scenario.

Applications of URL Rewriting Middleware:

Here are some common scenarios where URL rewriting might be beneficial:

- **Migrating to a new URL structure:** When you change the way URLs are structured in your application, you can use rewrites to redirect users from old URLs to the new ones.

- **Creating SEO-friendly URLs:** Rewriting can help you create URLs that are more descriptive and include relevant keywords for search engines.

- **Mapping legacy URLs:** If your application has been around for a while, you might have old URLs that you still want to support. Rewriting can help you map these old URLs to the new resources they point to.

- **Vanity URLs:** You can use rewrites to create custom, shorter URLs for specific resources in your application.

- **Content Management Systems (CMS):** Rewriting can be helpful in CMS systems where content URLs might not be user-friendly by default.

Example:

Imagine you have a website with a product catalog. Originally, your product URLs might have looked like this:

- /products/1

- /products/2

However, you decide to improve the user experience by including the product name in the URL:

- /products/shirt

- /products/hat

Using URL rewriting, you can define rules to automatically rewrite the old URLs to the new format, ensuring users still reach the correct product pages even if they use the old links.

What are the Caching or Response Caching strategies in ASP.NET Core?

Caching is a crucial performance optimization technique in ASP.NET Core applications. It involves storing frequently accessed data in a temporary location for faster retrieval, reducing the load on your server and improving response times for users. ASP.NET Core offers two primary caching strategies:

1. In-Memory Caching:

- **Mechanism:** Stores cached data in the server's main memory (RAM) for fast access.

- **Benefits:**

    ○ Fastest caching option due to in-memory storage.

    ○ Ideal for frequently accessed, static data that doesn't change frequently.

- **Drawbacks:**

    ○ Data is lost when the server restarts or if memory pressure forces eviction.

    ○ Not suitable for large datasets due to memory limitations.

Implementation:

ASP.NET Core provides the IMemoryCache interface for in-memory caching. You can use this interface to store and retrieve data from the cache:

```
public class HomeController : Controller
{
```

```
private readonly IMemoryCache _cache;

public HomeController(IMemoryCache cache)

{

_cache = cache;

}

public IActionResult

Index()

{

string cachedData;

if (!_cache.TryGetValue("greeting", out cachedData))

{

cachedData = "Hello from ASP.NET Core!";

_cache.Set("greeting", cachedData, TimeSpan.FromMinutes(10)); //
Set expiration

}

return View(cachedData);

}

}
```

2. Response Caching:

- **Mechanism:** Configures the server to cache the entire HTTP response, including headers and body, for a specified duration. Caching can be implemented at the server or client level (browser cache).

- **Benefits:**

    ○ Can cache dynamic content, not just static data, depending on the configuration.

- ○ Reduces server load for frequently accessed resources.

- **Drawbacks:**

  - ○ Requires careful configuration to avoid caching dynamic content that changes frequently.

  - ○ Relies on HTTP headers for client-side caching, which might be ignored by browsers depending on user settings.

Implementation:

ASP.NET Core offers various ways to implement response caching:

- **[ResponseCache] Attribute:** Decorates controller actions to define caching behavior like duration and cache invalidation strategies.

- **Response Caching Middleware:** Allows more granular control over caching logic for specific routes or responses.

Choosing the Right Caching Strategy:

The best caching strategy depends on the type of data you want to cache and its update frequency:

- Use in-memory caching for frequently accessed, static data that changes infrequently.

- Use response caching for dynamic content with predictable changes or content that doesn't change frequently. However, be cautious and use appropriate cache invalidation strategies to avoid stale data.

Additional Considerations:

- **Cache Expiration:** Implement cache expiration mechanisms to ensure cached data is refreshed periodically when it becomes outdated.

- **Cache Invalidation:** Define strategies to invalidate cached data when the underlying data source changes.

- **Cache Busting:** Use techniques like query string parameters or versioning to force browsers to fetch the latest version of a resource if the content has changed.

Difference between In-memory and Distributed caching in ASP.NET Core.

Both In-memory and Distributed caching are techniques for storing and retrieving data in ASP.NET Core applications, but they differ in terms of storage location, scalability, and suitability for various scenarios.

In-memory Caching:

- **Storage:** Data is stored in the server's main memory (RAM) for fast access.

- **Benefits:**

  - Fastest caching option due to in-memory storage.

  - Ideal for frequently accessed, static data that doesn't change frequently.

  - Simpler to implement compared to distributed caching.

- **Drawbacks:**

  - Data is lost when the server restarts or if memory pressure forces eviction.

  - Not suitable for large datasets due to memory limitations.

  - Not scalable beyond a single server.

Distributed Caching:

- **Storage:** Data is stored on a dedicated cache server or service external to the web application server. This can be a Redis server, Azure Cache for Redis, or any other distributed cache solution.

- **Benefits:**

  - Data survives server restarts.

  - Scales horizontally by adding more cache servers to handle increased load.

  - Enables sharing cached data across multiple web servers in a web farm environment.

- **Drawbacks:**

  - Slower access compared to in-memory caching due to network overhead in communication with the cache server.

  - More complex to implement and manage compared to in-memory caching.

  - Introduces additional dependencies on the external cache service.

Choosing the Right Caching Strategy:

The choice between in-memory and distributed caching depends on your application's specific needs:

- **Use In-memory caching for:**

  - Frequently accessed, static data that changes infrequently.

  - Simple web applications with limited data needs and a single server.

  - Scenarios where fast access is crucial, even if data might be lost on restarts.

- **Use Distributed caching for:**

  - Large datasets that wouldn't fit comfortably in server memory.

  - Web applications deployed in a web farm environment where cached data needs to be shared across servers.

- ○ Scenarios where data survival across server restarts is important.

Here's a table summarizing the key differences:

How to enable Cross-Origin Requests (CORS) in AS P.NET Core for API access from different domains?

By default, web browsers enforce the Same-Origin Policy (SOP) to prevent malicious scripts from accessing resources from different domains. This can be a hurdle when developing APIs in ASP.NET Core that need to be accessed by applications running on different domains (cross-origin requests).

Here's how to enable Cross-Origin Requests (CORS) in ASP.NET Core to allow controlled access to your API from different origins:

1. Using the AddCors service:

This is the recommended approach for configuring CORS policies in ASP.NET Core. You can configure CORS in your Startup.cs file:

public void ConfigureServices(IServiceCollection services)

{

// ... other service registrations

services.AddCors(options =>

{

options.AddPolicy("MyPolicy", builder =>

{

builder.WithOrigins("https://alloweddomain1.com", "https://allowed domain2.com")

.AllowAnyMethod()

.AllowAnyHeader();

```
// You can configure origins, methods, headers, and credentials as needed

});

});

}
```

Explanation:

- AddCors service is used to register CORS policies.

- Define a new policy named "MyPolicy" using AddPolicy.

- Configure the policy using a builder lambda:

  - WithOrigins: Specify allowed origins for cross-origin requests.

  - AllowAnyMethod: Allow all HTTP methods (GET, POST, PUT, DELETE, etc.) for requests under this policy (optional, you can specify specific methods).

  - AllowAnyHeader: Allow all request headers (optional, you can specify specific allowed headers).

2. Enabling CORS in Middleware:

Alternatively, you can use middleware to configure CORS globally or for specific routes. However, the AddCors service approach is generally preferred for better separation of concerns.

3. Applying the Policy:

Once you have defined your CORS policy, you need to apply it to your controllers or specific actions:

```
public class MyController : Controller

{

[HttpGet]

[Route("api/data")]
```

[EnableCors("MyPolicy")] // Apply the "MyPolicy" CORS policy to this action

public IActionResult GetMyData()

{

// ... your API logic

}

}

Explanation:

- Decorate the desired controller action with the [EnableCors("MyPolicy")] attribute to apply the previously defined "MyPolicy" CORS policy.

Additional Considerations:

- **Origin Specificity:** It's generally recommended to be specific about allowed origins to enhance security. Don't use AllowAnyOrigin in production environments unless necessary.

- **Allowed Methods and Headers:** Configure allowed methods and headers based on your API's needs. Allowing unnecessary methods or headers can introduce security vulnerabilities.

- **Credentials:** By default, CORS requests don't send cookies or authorization headers. If your API requires credentials, you need to explicitly allow them using AllowCredentials in your policy configuration.

Describe strongly typed views and their benefits in ASP.NET Core MVC.

In ASP.NET Core MVC, strongly typed views offer a significant advantage over loosely typed views. Here's a breakdown of both approaches and the benefits of using strongly typed views:

1. Loosely Typed Views: Data Access: Use ViewData or ViewBag dynamic properties on the controller to pass data to the view.

Example:

```
// Controller

public IActionResult Index()

{

ViewData["Message"] = "Hello from ASP.NET Core!";

return View();

}

// View (cshtml)

<h1>@ViewData["Message"]</h1>
```

- **Drawbacks:**

    - Prone to typos and errors at runtime, as the view doesn't explicitly know the data type it's working with.

    - IntelliSense and code completion support are limited in the view.

    - Tightly coupled view to the controller data structure. Changing the data structure in the controller might require view modifications.

2. Strongly Typed Views: Model Binding: Pass a specific model object as the view model to the view.

Example:

```
// ViewModel

public class MyViewModel

{
```

```
public string Message { get; set; }

}

// Controller

public IActionResult Index()

{

var model = new MyViewModel { Message = "Hello from ASP.NET
Core!" };

return View(model);

}

// View (cshtml)

<h1>@Model.Message</h1>
```

- **Benefits:**

  - **Type Safety:** Explicitly defines the type of data the view
    expects, reducing runtime errors caused by typos or data
    type mismatches.

  - **Improved IntelliSense:** Code completion and auto-sug-
    gestions within the view benefit from knowing the model
    type.

  - **Loose Coupling:** Changes in the controller data structure
    might not necessarily require view modifications as long as
    the model properties remain compatible.

  - **Clearer Code:** Enhances code readability and maintain-
    ability by explicitly defining data types used in the view.

Additional Advantages of Strongly Typed Views:

- **Model Validation:** You can leverage data annotation attributes
  on the model class to implement validation logic, ensuring data
  integrity before processing it further.

- **Testability:** Strongly typed views are generally easier to unit test due to their well-defined data types and separation from controller logic.

Choosing Between Loosely and Strongly Typed Views:

- **Simple Views with Limited Data:** For very basic views with minimal data requirements, loosely typed views might suffice.

- **Complex Views with Structured Data:** For any view displaying or interacting with complex data structures, strongly typed views are the recommended approach due to their type safety, improved developer experience, and testability benefits.

CHAPTER 6

— · —

EF CORE

What is Entity Framework Core and how does it differ from Entity Framework?

Entity Framework Core (EF Core) is a lightweight and extensible object-relational mapper (ORM) framework for .NET Core applications. It provides a way to interact with relational databases using object-oriented programming concepts, simplifying data access and reducing boilerplate code.

Key differences between EF Core and Entity Framework:

- **Platform Independence:** EF Core is designed to be cross-platform, supporting various databases like SQL Server, PostgreSQL, MySQL, SQLite, and more. In contrast, Entity Framework was primarily focused on SQL Server.

- **Lightweight and Modular:** EF Core is built as a modular framework, allowing you to select only the components you need, making it more efficient and adaptable to different scenarios.

- **Improved Performance:** EF Core offers performance improvements, especially in certain scenarios like query execution and change tracking.

- **Asynchronous Programming:** EF Core supports asynchronous programming, enabling more efficient use of resources and better responsiveness in modern applications.

- **Simplified Configuration:** EF Core provides a simplified configuration experience using tools like dependency injection and configuration files.

- **Convention-based Configuration:** EF Core encourages convention-based configuration, reducing the need for explicit mapping in many cases.

- **Extensibility:** EF Core is highly extensible, allowing you to customize its behavior through plugins and extensions.

Key features of Entity Framework Core:

- **Code First:** Define your domain model using C# classes, and EF Core will automatically generate the corresponding database schema.

- **Database First:** Create your database schema and use EF Core to generate entity classes from the existing schema.

- **Model-View-Controller (MVC):** EF Core integrates seamlessly with ASP.NET Core MVC, providing a powerful framework for building web applications.

- **LINQ:** Use LINQ to query your database using a familiar syntax, making data retrieval and manipulation easier.

- **Change Tracking:** EF Core automatically tracks changes made to your entities, simplifying data persistence and updates.

- **Migrations:** EF Core provides a tool to manage database schema changes over time, making it easier to evolve your application's data model.

What are the different approaches to database schema generation in EF Core?

Entity Framework Core (EF Core) offers three primary approaches to database schema generation:

1. Code First:

- **Process:** You define your domain model using C# classes, and EF Core automatically generates the corresponding database schema based on the model.

- **Benefits:**

  - Most flexible approach, allowing you to define your model and database schema in code.

  - Ideal for new applications or when you want to start with a clean slate.

  - Supports migrations for managing database schema changes over time.

- **Drawbacks:**

  - Requires more upfront effort to define the entire model.

  - Might not be suitable for large, complex existing databases.

2. Database First:

- **Process:** You create your database schema using a database management tool, and EF Core generates entity classes based on the existing schema.

- **Benefits:**

  - Ideal for existing databases that you need to integrate with your application.

  - Minimal upfront effort required to define the model.

- **Drawbacks:**

  - Less flexible than Code First, as you're constrained by the existing schema.

  - Might require manual adjustments to the generated entity classes if the schema changes.

3. Model First:

- **Process:** You design your data model using a visual designer tool (e.g., EF Core Power Tools), and EF Core generates both the entity classes and the database schema.

- **Benefits:**

  - Provides a visual approach to designing your data model.

  - Can be useful for teams with a mix of developers and database administrators.

- **Drawbacks:**

  - Requires a visual design tool and might not be as flexible as Code First.

Choosing the Right Approach:

The best approach depends on your specific needs and preferences:

- **New applications:** Code First is often the preferred choice, as it provides the most flexibility and allows you to define your model from the beginning.

- **Existing databases:** Database First is a good option for integrating with existing databases.

- **Visual design:** Model First can be useful if you prefer a visual approach to designing your data model.

You can also combine these approaches in some scenarios. For example, you might start with Database First for an existing database and then use Code First to extend the model or make changes.

Additional Considerations:

- **Migrations:** Regardless of the approach you choose, EF Core provides migrations to manage database schema changes over time.

- **Reverse Engineering:** You can use EF Core's reverse engineering tools to generate entity classes from an existing database schema, even if you started with Code First.

How does EF Core handle change tracking and entity state management?

Entity Framework Core (EF Core) employs a robust change tracking mechanism to monitor changes made to your entities and efficiently update the database when necessary. This feature significantly simplifies data persistence and reduces boilerplate code.

Change Tracking Process:

1. **Entity Creation:** When you create a new entity instance, EF Core automatically sets its state to Added. This indicates that the entity needs to be inserted into the database.

2. **Entity Modification:** If you modify the properties of an existing entity, EF Core sets its state to Modified. This signals that the entity needs to be updated in the database.

3. **Entity Deletion:** When you mark an entity for deletion, EF Core sets its state to Deleted. This indicates that the entity should be removed from the database.

Entity State Management:

EF Core maintains an internal state for each entity, tracking changes made to its properties. This information is used to determine which actions need to be taken when you call SaveChanges on the DbContext instance.

Key Entity States:

- **Added:** The entity is new and needs to be inserted into the database.

- **Modified:** The entity has been modified and needs to be updated in the database.

- **Deleted:** The entity has been marked for deletion and needs to be removed from the database.

- **Unchanged:** The entity has not been modified since it was loaded from the database.

- **Detached:** The entity is no longer tracked by EF Core, meaning any changes made to it will not be persisted to the database.

Change Tracking Strategies:

EF Core offers different change tracking strategies to optimize performance based on your application's needs:

- **Change Tracking Proxies:** The default strategy, which uses proxies to intercept property accesses and track changes.

- **Snapshot:** Tracks changes by storing a snapshot of the original values when an entity is loaded.

- **Client-Side Set-Based:** Tracks changes in a set-based manner, which can be more efficient for large datasets.

Key Considerations:

- **Performance:** The choice of change tracking strategy can impact performance. Consider your application's specific needs and test different strategies to find the optimal one.

- **Entity State Queries:** You can use methods like Entry(entity).State to retrieve the current state of an entity and perform actions based on its state.

- **Manual State Management:** In some cases, you might need to manually set the state of an entity if EF Core's automatic tracking doesn't meet your requirements.

Explain the role of the DbContext class in EF Core.

The DbContext class is a fundamental component of Entity Framework Core (EF Core). It serves as the primary entry point for interacting with your database and managing your entity data.

Key responsibilities of the DbContext class:

- **Represents a Unit of Work:** A DbContext represents a single unit of work within a database transaction. This means that all changes made to entities within a DbContext instance are tracked and persisted in a single atomic operation.

- **Manages Entity Lifetimes:** The DbContext tracks the state of entities (Added, Modified, Deleted) and manages their persistence to the database.

- **Provides Querying Capabilities:** You use the DbContext instance to execute LINQ queries against your entities, retrieving data from the database based on your criteria.

- **Handles Database Connections:** The DbContext manages the connection to your database, ensuring that connections are opened and closed as needed.

- **Supports Change Tracking:** The DbContext automatically tracks changes made to your entities, allowing you to efficiently persist data to the database.

- **Integrates with Dependency Injection:** EF Core integrates seamlessly with ASP.NET Core's dependency injection system, making it easy to inject DbContext instances into your controllers, services, and other components.

Example:

```
public class MyDbContext : DbContext

{

public MyDbContext(DbContextOptions<MyDbContext> options) :
base(options)

{ }

public DbSet<Product> Products { get; set; }

}
```

In this example, MyDbContext is a custom DbContext class that defines a DbSet property named Products. This DbSet represents a collection of Product entities in the database.

Key points to remember:

- Each unit of work typically involves a single DbContext instance.

- You can use the SaveChanges method on the DbContext to persist changes made to your entities to the database.

- The DbContext can be configured using the DbContextOptions class to specify things like the connection string and database provider.

- It's important to use a dependency injection container to manage the lifetime of DbContext instances, ensuring they are disposed of properly when no longer needed.

How LINQ is used in EF Core?

LINQ (Language-Integrated Query) is a powerful feature in Entity Framework Core (EF Core) that allows you to query your database using a syntax similar to C# language constructs. This makes data retrieval and manipulation much more intuitive and easier to read.

Here's a breakdown of how LINQ is used with EF Core:

1. Querying Data:

- You can use LINQ to query your entities in a way that's natural to C# developers.

- Common LINQ operators include Where, Select, Join, GroupBy, OrderBy, and many others.

Here's a simple example:

var products = _context.Products.Where(p => p.Price > 100).ToList();

This query retrieves all products from the database with a price greater than 100.

2. Projecting Data:

- You can project your query results into new types or anonymous objects using Select.

- This allows you to customize the data returned from your queries.

```
var productNames = _context.Products.Select(p => p.Name).ToList();
```

3. Joining Data:

- LINQ supports joining related entities using Join or GroupJoin operators.

- This enables you to retrieve data from multiple tables based on relationships between entities.

```
var productsWithCategories = _context.Products

.Join(_context.Categories,

p => p.CategoryId,

c => c.Id,

(p, c) => new { Product = p, Category = c })

.ToList();
```

4. Filtering Data:

- Use Where to filter results based on specific conditions.

- You can combine multiple conditions using logical operators (&&, ||, !).

```
var expensiveProducts = _context.Products.Where(p => p.Price > 1000
&& p.IsAvailable).ToList();
```

5. Grouping Data: Group data using GroupBy to aggregate results based on specific criteria.

```
var productsByCategory = _context.Products

.GroupBy(p => p.Category)

.Select(g => new { Category = g.Key, ProductCount = g.Count() })
```

.ToList();

6. Ordering Data: Use OrderBy, OrderByDescending, ThenBy, and ThenByDescending to sort results based on specific properties.

var productsByPrice = _context.Products.OrderBy(p => p.Price).ToList();

7. Asynchronous Queries: EF Core supports asynchronous queries using ToListAsync and other asynchronous methods. This is important for performance and responsiveness in modern applications.

var productsAsync = await _context.Products.ToListAsync();

Additional Features:

- **Deferred Execution:** LINQ queries in EF Core are typically deferred, meaning they are not executed until you iterate over the results.

- **Customizable Query Providers:** You can create custom query providers to integrate with different data sources or modify query behavior.

How does EF Core handle relationships between entities?

Entity Framework Core (EF Core) provides a robust mechanism for handling relationships between entities, allowing you to model complex data structures and relationships in your application. Here's a breakdown of how EF Core handles different types of relationships:

1. One-to-Many Relationships:

- In a one-to-many relationship, one entity can be associated with many entities of another type.

- For example, a Customer entity can have many Order entities.

- To represent this relationship in EF Core, you define a navigation property on the "many" side (e.g., Customer.Orders) and use a foreign key property on the "many" side to reference the "one" side.

2. Many-to-Many Relationships:

- In a many-to-many relationship, both entities can have multiple associations with each other.

- For example, a Product can be associated with many Category entities, and a Category can have many Product entities.

- EF Core creates a join table to represent this relationship. You define navigation properties on both sides of the relationship, and EF Core automatically manages the join table.

3. One-to-One Relationships:

- In a one-to-one relationship, one entity can be associated with at most one entity of another type, and vice versa.

- For example, a Person entity can have one Address entity.

- You can represent this relationship using a foreign key on either side of the relationship, or by using a shared primary key if the relationship is mandatory.

Key Concepts and Configuration:

- **Navigation Properties:** These properties allow you to navigate between related entities in your code. For example, you can use Customer.Orders to access the orders associated with a customer.

- **Foreign Keys:** Foreign keys are used to establish relationships between entities. EF Core can automatically configure foreign keys based on naming conventions or you can explicitly define them.

- **Fluent API:** You can use the Fluent API to customize relationship configuration, including setting cascade delete behavior, specifying foreign key properties, and customizing navigation property names.

Example:

public class Customer

{

public int Id { get; set; }

public string Name { get; set; }

public ICollection<Order> Orders { get; set; }

}

public class Order

{

public int Id { get; set; }

public int CustomerId { get; set; } // Foreign key

public Customer Customer { get; set; }

}

What are migrations in EF Core and how are they used to manage database schema changes?

Migrations in Entity Framework Core (EF Core) are a powerful tool for managing database schema changes over time. They allow you to evolve your database schema incrementally and track changes to your model in a controlled and repeatable way.

Key features and benefits of migrations:

- **Version Control:** Migrations are like version control for your database schema. Each migration represents a specific change to the schema, making it easy to track and manage changes.

- **Automatic Schema Updates:** When you apply a migration, EF Core automatically updates the database schema to match the changes defined in the migration.

- **Reversibility:** Migrations can be reversed, allowing you to roll back changes if necessary.

- **Dependency Tracking:** EF Core tracks dependencies between migrations, ensuring that migrations are applied in the correct order.

- **Integration with Code First:** Migrations are tightly integrated with the Code First approach, making it easy to manage schema changes alongside your model definitions.

How to use migrations:

1. **Create a Migration:** Use the Add-Migration command in the Package Manager Console or dotnet CLI to create a new migration. This will generate a migration class and a snapshot of the current database schema.

2. **Make Changes:** Modify the Up and Down methods in the migration class to define the database schema changes. The Up method applies the changes, while the Down method reverts them.

3. **Apply the Migration:** Use the Update-Database command to apply the migration to your database. This will update the schema to match the changes defined in the migration.

Example:

```csharp
public partial class AddProductTable : Migration

{

protected override void Up(MigrationBuilder migrationBuilder)

{

migrationBuilder.CreateTable(name: "Products", table =>

{

table.PrimaryKey("PK_Products", x => x.Id);

table.Column<int>("Id", nullable: false)
```

```
.Annotation("SqlServer:Identity", "1, 1");

table.Column<string>("Name", nullable: false);

table.Column<decimal>("Price", nullable: false);

});

}

protected override void Down(MigrationBuilder migrationBuilder)

{

migrationBuilder.DropTable(name: "Products");

}

}
```

This migration creates a new table named Products with columns for Id, Name, and Price. You can then apply this migration to your database using the Update-Database command.

Additional features of migrations:

- **Data Seeding:** You can include data seeding in migrations to populate your database with initial data.

- **Custom Operations:** You can perform custom operations in migrations, such as executing raw SQL commands or creating stored procedures.

- **Migration Rollbacks:** You can use the Update-Database -TargetMigration command to roll back to a specific migration.

How does EF Core support asynchronous programming?

Entity Framework Core (EF Core) provides robust support for asynchronous programming, making it well-suited for modern applications that require efficient handling of long-running tasks and I/O operations. This support is essential for building responsive and scalable applications.

How to use asynchronous programming with EF Core:

- **Asynchronous Methods:** EF Core provides asynchronous methods for most operations, such as ToListAsync, FirstOrDefaultAsync, SaveChangesAsync, and more.

- **Await Keyword:** Use the await keyword to asynchronously wait for the completion of these methods.

- **Async/Await Pattern:** Follow the async/await pattern to write asynchronous code in a more readable and maintainable way.

Example:

```
public async Task<IActionResult> GetProductsAsync()

{

var products = await _context.Products.ToListAsync();

return View(products);

}
```

In this example, the ToListAsync method is used to asynchronously retrieve a list of products from the database. The await keyword ensures that the controller action waits for the query to complete before returning the result.

Additional Considerations:

- **Asynchronous DbContext:** Create a DbContext instance using DbContextOptionsBuilder.UseSqlServer(connectionString).Options to enable asynchronous operations.

- **Asynchronous Dependency Injection:** Register your DbContext as an asynchronous service in your Startup.cs file.

- **Asynchronous Middleware:** If you're using custom middleware, ensure it's also asynchronous to avoid blocking the request pipeline.

How do you configure EF Core to use different database providers?

Configuring EF Core to use different database providers involves a few key steps:

Install the Required NuGet Package:

- For SQL Server: Microsoft.EntityFrameworkCore.SqlServer

- For PostgreSQL: Npgsql.EntityFrameworkCore.PostgreSQL

- For MySQL: MySql.Data.EntityFrameworkCore

- For SQLite: Microsoft.EntityFrameworkCore.Sqlite

- And so on for other supported providers.

Register the Provider in Startup.cs: Use the AddDbContext extension method in the ConfigureServices method of your Startup.cs file to register the DbContext with the appropriate provider:

```
public void ConfigureServices(IServiceCollection services)

{

services.AddDbContext<MyDbContext>(options =>

{

options.UseSqlServer("YourConnectionString");

// Replace with your connection string

});

}
```

Specify Connection String: Provide the connection string for your database in the UseSqlServer, UseNpgsql, UseMySQL, or UseSqlite method. You can obtain the connection string from your database management system or configuration file.

Example:

public void ConfigureServices(IServiceCollection services)

{

services.AddDbContext<MyDbContext>(options =>

{

options.UseSqlServer("Server=your-server;Database=your-database;Tr usted_Connection=True;");

});

}

Additional Considerations:

- **NuGet Package Versions:** Ensure you're using compatible versions of the EF Core provider and the database driver.

- **Configuration Sources:** You can use configuration sources like environment variables, appsettings.json files, or Azure Key Vault to store your connection string securely.

- **Multiple Providers:** If your application needs to support multiple databases, you can conditionally register the provider based on environment variables or other criteria.

- **Custom Providers:** For advanced scenarios, you can create custom providers to integrate with non-supported databases.

What are some common EF Core configuration options and their uses?

Entity Framework Core (EF Core) provides various configuration options to tailor its behavior and performance according to your specific needs. Here are some common options and their uses:

Connection String: Purpose: Specifies the connection information to your database.

Example:services.AddDbContext<MyDbContext>(options =>

{

options.UseSqlServer("Server=your-server;Database=your-database;Trusted_Connection=True;");

});

Query Filters: Purpose: Apply global filters to all queries executed by the DbContext.

Example:services.AddDbContext<MyDbContext>(options =>

{

options.UseSqlServer("YourConnectionString") .UseQueryTracking-Behavior(QueryTrackingBehavior.NoTracking)

.AddQueryFilter(p => !p.IsDeleted);

});

Lazy Loading: Purpose: Controls whether related entities are loaded automatically when a parent entity is accessed.

Example:services.AddDbContext<MyDbContext>(options =>

{

options.UseSqlServer("YourConnectionString")

.UseLazyLoadingProxies();

});

Change Tracking Behavior: Purpose: Determines how EF Core tracks changes to entities.

Example:services.AddDbContext<MyDbContext>(options =>

{

options.UseSqlServer("YourConnectionString") .UseQueryTracking-Behavior(QueryTrackingBehavior.NoTracking);

```
});
```

Command Interceptors: Purpose: Intercept and modify database commands before they are executed.

Example:services.AddDbContext<MyDbContext>(options =>

```
{

options.UseSqlServer("YourConnectionString")

.AddInterceptors(new MyCommandInterceptor());

});
```

Query Filters: Purpose: Apply global filters to all queries executed by the DbContext.

Example:services.AddDbContext<MyDbContext>(options =>

```
{

options.UseSqlServer("YourConnectionString")

.AddQueryFilter(p => !p.IsDeleted);

});
```

Logging: Purpose: Configure logging to track EF Core activities and diagnose issues.

Example:services.AddDbContext<MyDbContext>(options =>

```
{

options.UseSqlServer("YourConnectionString")

.LogToConsole(LogLevel.Information);

});
```

How do you handle lazy loading and eager loading of related entities in EF Core?

Lazy Loading:

- **Definition:** Related entities are not loaded from the database until they are accessed for the first time. This can improve performance in scenarios where you don't need all related entities immediately.

- **Mechanism:** EF Core uses proxies to intercept property accesses and load the related entities on demand.

Enabling Lazy Loading:services.AddDbContext<MyDbContext>(
options =>

{

options.UseSqlServer("YourConnectionString")

.UseLazyLoadingProxies();

});

Considerations:

- Can lead to multiple database trips if you access multiple related entities.

- Might not be suitable for scenarios where you need to load all related entities upfront.

Eager Loading:

- **Definition:** Related entities are loaded along with the parent entity in a single query.

- **Mechanism:** You explicitly include related entities in your query using the Include method.

Example:var productsWithCategories = _context.Products

.Include(p => p.Category)

.ToList();

Considerations:

- Can potentially load more data than necessary, leading to performance overhead.

- Use judiciously for scenarios where you know you need all related entities.

Choosing the Right Approach:

- **Lazy Loading:** Suitable for scenarios where you don't need all related entities immediately or when you want to optimize performance for cases where only a few related entities are accessed.

- **Eager Loading:** Use when you know you need all related entities upfront, as it can potentially reduce the number of database round trips.

Additional Tips:

- **Projection:** If you only need specific properties from related entities, use projection to select only the required columns and avoid unnecessary data loading.

- **Explicit Loading:** For more granular control, you can use explicit loading using the Entry method to load related entities on demand.

- **Performance Considerations:** Consider the performance implications of your choice based on your application's specific needs and the size of your datasets.

What are some techniques for improving EF Core query performance?

Here are some techniques to enhance the performance of your Entity Framework Core (EF Core) queries:

1. Avoid Unnecessary Data:

- **Projection:** Select only the necessary properties using the Select method to reduce the amount of data transferred.

- **Include vs. ThenInclude:** Use Include judiciously to eager load related entities only when needed. Avoid excessive eager loading.

2. Query Optimization:

- **Query Caching:** Consider using query caching for frequently executed queries.

- **Indexes:** Ensure appropriate indexes are created on frequently queried columns to improve query performance.

- **Join Optimization:** Analyze joins to avoid unnecessary data access and optimize query execution plans.

3. Batching and Bulk Operations:

- **Batching:** For multiple related operations, consider using batching techniques like AddRange or UpdateRange to reduce the number of round trips to the database.

- **Bulk Operations:** If you need to insert or update a large number of entities, explore bulk operations provided by your database provider for improved performance.

4. Asynchronous Programming:

- **Avoid Blocking:** Use asynchronous methods provided by EF Core to prevent blocking the main thread and improve responsiveness.

5. Connection Pooling:

- **Optimize Connections:** Ensure your connection pooling settings are configured correctly to reuse connections efficiently.

6. Query Execution Logging:

- **Analyze Queries:** Use EF Core's logging features to inspect generated SQL queries and identify performance bottlenecks.

7. Database Design:

- **Normalization:** Ensure your database schema is properly normalized to avoid redundancy and improve query performance.

- **Denormalization:** In certain cases, denormalizing data can improve query performance, but use this technique judiciously to avoid data inconsistencies.

8. Avoid Excessive Data Transfer:

- **Streaming:** For large datasets, consider using streaming techniques to process data in chunks, reducing memory usage.

9. Consider External Caching:

- **Distributed Caching:** Explore using distributed caching solutions like Redis or Memcached to cache frequently accessed data outside of your application.

10. Profiling and Benchmarking:

- **Identify Bottlenecks:** Use profiling tools to identify performance bottlenecks in your queries and application code.

- **Benchmarking:** Measure the performance of different query optimizations to determine their effectiveness.

How can you optimize EF Core change tracking behavior?

Entity Framework Core (EF Core) automatically tracks changes made to your entities, which is essential for persisting data to the database. However, change tracking can sometimes impact performance, especially in scenarios with large datasets or frequent updates. Here are some techniques to optimize change tracking behavior:

1. No Tracking:

- **Purpose:** Disable change tracking entirely for certain queries.

- **When to Use:** When you only need to read data from the database and don't need to modify entities.

Example:var products = _context.Products.AsNoTracking().ToList();

2. Detached Criteria: Purpose: Specify criteria to determine whether an entity should be tracked or detached.

Example:var product = _context.Products.AsNoTracking()

.Where(p => p.Id == 1)

.FirstOrDefault();

3. Change Tracking Proxies: Purpose: Enable lazy loading and change tracking using proxies.

Configuration:services.AddDbContext<MyDbContext>(options =>

{

options.UseSqlServer("YourConnectionString")

.UseLazyLoadingProxies();

});

Considerations:

- Can introduce performance overhead for complex scenarios.

- Consider disabling proxies if you don't need lazy loading.

4. Snapshot Change Tracking: Purpose: Stores a snapshot of the original values when an entity is loaded, making change tracking more efficient for certain scenarios.

Configuration:services.AddDbContext<MyDbContext>(options =>

{

options.UseSqlServer("YourConnectionString") .UseQueryTracking-Behavior(QueryTrackingBehavior.NoTracking);

});

Considerations: Might not be suitable for scenarios where you need to track changes made to nested properties.

5. Client-Side Set-Based Change Tracking: Purpose: Tracks changes in a set-based manner, which can be more efficient for large datasets.

Configuration:services.AddDbContext<MyDbContext>(options =>

{

options.UseSqlServer("YourConnectionString")   .UseQueryTrack-ingBehavior(QueryTrackingBehavior.NoTracking)

.UseClientSetTracking();

});

Considerations: Might have limitations for certain scenarios, such as tracking changes to nested properties.

6. Manual State Management: Purpose: Manually set the entity state to Added, Modified, or Deleted for more granular control.

Example:var product = _context.Products.Find(1);

product.Name = "New Name";

_context.Entry(product).State = EntityState.Modified;

await _context.SaveChangesAsync();

7. Avoid Unnecessary Updates:

- **Check for Changes:** Before calling SaveChanges, check if any changes have actually been made to the entity.

- **Conditional Updates:** Use conditional updates in your queries to avoid unnecessary updates.

What are the benefits of using raw SQL queries with EF Core?

Using raw SQL queries with Entity Framework Core (EF Core) can provide certain benefits, especially in specific scenarios:

Performance Optimization:

Direct Control: Raw SQL queries allow you to write custom SQL statements optimized for your database engine, potentially leading to better performance.

Complex Queries: For highly complex queries that are difficult to express using LINQ, raw SQL can provide more flexibility and control.

Database-Specific Features:

Leverage Vendor-Specific Features: Raw SQL queries enable you to utilize database-specific features or functions that might not be directly supported by EF Core's LINQ-to-Entities provider.

Legacy Systems:

Integration: If you're working with legacy systems or stored procedures, raw SQL queries might be necessary to interact with existing database logic.

Performance Analysis:

Profiling: Raw SQL queries can be helpful for profiling and analyzing query performance, identifying bottlenecks, and optimizing your database interactions.

Third-Party Libraries:

Integration: Some third-party libraries or frameworks might require raw SQL queries for specific functionality or integrations.

However, there are also some considerations when using raw SQL queries:

- **Reduced Type Safety:** Raw SQL queries can bypass EF Core's type safety mechanisms, potentially leading to runtime errors if you're not careful.

- **Maintainability:** Using raw SQL can make your code less maintainable, especially if the SQL is complex or difficult to understand.

- **Abstraction Layer:** EF Core's LINQ-to-Entities provider provides a layer of abstraction that can simplify data access and make your code more portable.

How does EF Core handle entity inheritance?

Entity Framework Core (EF Core) provides robust support for entity inheritance, allowing you to model complex relationships between entities and leverage polymorphism effectively. Here are the different approaches you can use:

1. Table per Hierarchy (TPH):

- **Concept:** All entities in the inheritance hierarchy are stored in a single table. A discriminator column is used to differentiate between the different types of entities.

- **Benefits:**

  - Simplest approach to implement.

  - Requires fewer database tables.

- **Drawbacks:**

  - Can lead to null values for properties that are specific to derived types.

  - Might not be the most efficient approach for large hierarchies.

2. Table per Concrete Type (TPC):

- **Concept:** Each concrete entity type has its own table.

- **Benefits:**

- ◦ Avoids null values for properties specific to derived types.

- ◦ Can be more efficient for large hierarchies.

- **Drawbacks:** Requires more database tables.

3. Table per Type (TPT):

- **Concept:** Similar to TPT, but includes a base table for common properties shared by all derived entities.

- **Benefits:** Combines the advantages of TPH and TPC.

- **Drawbacks:** Requires more database tables than TPH.

Choosing the Right Approach:

The best approach depends on your specific requirements and the nature of your inheritance hierarchy. Consider the following factors:

- **Performance:** TPT can be more efficient for large hierarchies, while TPH might be simpler for smaller hierarchies.

- **Data Integrity:** TPT avoids null values for type-specific properties, which can improve data integrity.

- **Flexibility:** TPH offers more flexibility in terms of querying and modifying entities, as all entities are stored in a single table.

Example (TPH):

```
public abstract class Person

{

public int Id { get; set; }

public string Name { get; set; }

public string Discriminator { get; set; } // Used to differentiate types

}

public class Student : Person
```

```csharp
{
public string Grade { get; set; }
}
public class Teacher : Person
{
public string Subject { get; set; }
}
```

Example (TPT):

```csharp
public abstract class Person
{
public int Id { get; set; }
public string Name { get; set; }
}
public class Student : Person
{
public string Grade { get; set; }
}
public class Teacher : Person
{
public string Subject { get; set; }
}
```

What is shadow property mapping in EF Core?

Shadow property mapping in Entity Framework Core (EF Core) allows you to define properties in your entity classes that do not have corresponding columns in the database. These properties can be used for various purposes, such as:

- **Calculated Properties:** Deriving values from other properties within the entity.

- **Temporary Storage:** Storing intermediate values during data processing.

- **Custom Mapping:** Mapping properties to database columns with different names or data types.

Key benefits of shadow property mapping:

- **Improved Code Organization:** Keeps your entity classes clean and focused on the core domain model.

- **Flexibility:** Provides flexibility in defining custom properties and mapping them to database columns.

- **Separation of Concerns:** Separates data access and business logic concerns, making your code more maintainable.

How to use shadow property mapping:

1. **Define the Shadow Property:** Create a property in your entity class without applying any data annotations or mapping conventions.

2. **Configure the Mapping:** Use the Fluent API in your DbContext class to configure the mapping for the shadow property. Specify the column name, data type, and any other relevant properties.

Example:

public class Product

```
{

public int Id { get; set; }

public string Name { get; set; }

public decimal CalculatedPrice { get; private set; }

}

protected override void OnModelCreating(ModelBuilder model-
Builder)

{

modelBuilder.Entity<Product>()

.Property(p => p.CalculatedPrice)

.HasComputedColumnSql("[Price] * 1.1");

}
```

In this example, CalculatedPrice is a shadow property that is calculated based on the Price property. The HasComputedColumnSql method is used to define the computed column expression in the database.

Additional Considerations:

- **Shadow Properties and Data Annotations:** Shadow properties cannot be directly decorated with data annotations. You need to use the Fluent API to configure their mapping.

- **Performance:** Be mindful of the performance implications of using shadow properties, especially if they involve complex calculations or database interactions.

- **Database Compatibility:** Ensure that your database supports computed columns or other mechanisms required for shadow property mapping.

Explain the concept of interception in EF Core.

Interception in Entity Framework Core (EF Core) is a powerful mechanism that allows you to intercept and modify database commands before they are executed. This provides flexibility for customizing behavior, logging, performance analysis, and implementing custom logic.

Key features and benefits of interception:

- **Customization:** Intercept and modify database commands to implement custom logic, such as auditing, logging, or security checks.

- **Performance Analysis:** Use interception to profile database queries and identify performance bottlenecks.

- **Debugging:** Monitor database interactions and debug issues more effectively.

- **Integration with Third-Party Libraries:** Integrate with third-party libraries that require intercepting database commands.

How to use interception:

1. **Create a Command Interceptor:** Implement the IDbCommandInterceptor interface to define the interception logic.

2. **Register the Interceptor:** Register the interceptor in your DbContext configuration using the AddInterceptors method.

Example:

```
public class MyCommandInterceptor : IDbCommandInterceptor

{

public void ReaderExecuting(DbCommand command, DbCommandReaderEventArgs eventArgs)

{
```

```
// Log the SQL query

Console.WriteLine(command.CommandText);

}

// Implement other methods as needed

}

public void ConfigureServices(IServiceCollection services)

{

services.AddDbContext<MyDbContext>(options =>

{

options.UseSqlServer("YourConnectionString")

.AddInterceptors(new MyCommandInterceptor());

});

}
```

Interception Methods:

- ReaderExecuting: Called before the command reader starts executing.

- ReaderExecuted: Called after the command reader has executed.

- NonQueryExecuting: Called before a non-query command is executed.

- NonQueryExecuted: Called after a non-query command has executed.

- ScalarExecuting: Called before a scalar command is executed.

- ScalarExecuted: Called after a scalar command has executed.

Additional Considerations:

- **Performance Impact:** Interception can introduce overhead, so use it judiciously.

- **Custom Logic:** Implement your custom logic within the interceptor methods to achieve the desired behavior.

- **Debugging:** Interception can be helpful for debugging database-related issues by logging or examining the intercepted commands.

How do you handle data seeding and initialization in EF Core?

Data Seeding in Entity Framework Core (EF Core) is the process of populating your database with initial data when the application starts. This is useful for setting up default values, creating test data, or initializing reference data.

Here's how you can handle data seeding in EF Core:

1. Create a Seed Method:

- Create a static method within your DbContext class or a separate class to encapsulate the seeding logic.

- The method should take an IServiceProvider as a parameter to access other services if needed.

2. Use the OnModelCreating Method: Override the OnModelCreating method in your DbContext class and call your seed method within it.

Example:

public class MyDbContext : DbContext

{

public DbSet<Product> Products { get; set; }

protected override void OnModelCreating(ModelBuilder modelBuilder)

```
{

SeedInitialData(modelBuilder);

}

private static void SeedInitialData(ModelBuilder modelBuilder)

{

modelBuilder.Entity<Product>().HasData(

new Product { Id = 1, Name = "Product 1", Price = 10.99},

new Product { Id = 2, Name = "Product 2", Price = 29.99}

);

}

}
```

3. Apply the Migration:

- Run the Update-Database command in the Package Manager Console or dotnet CLI to apply the migration that contains the seeding logic. This will populate the database with the initial data.

CHAPTER 7

WEB API & REST API

What is Web API?

A web API (Application Programming Interface) is a software interface that allows applications to communicate with each other over the internet. It provides a set of rules and protocols that define how applications can interact and exchange data.

Key characteristics of web APIs:

- **Platform-independent:** Web APIs can be accessed and used by applications running on different platforms (e.g., Windows, Linux, macOS).

- **Language-independent:** Web APIs can be consumed by applications written in different programming languages (e.g., C#, Java, Python).

- **Protocol-based:** Web APIs typically use HTTP as the underlying protocol, but other protocols can also be used.

- **RESTful:** Many modern web APIs follow the RESTful architecture style, which emphasizes simplicity, scalability, and statelessness.

Common use cases for web APIs:

- **Data access:** Providing access to data from databases or other data sources.

- **Integration:** Integrating different applications or systems.

- **Third-party services:** Offering services to other applications, such as payment processing, geolocation, or social media integration.

- **Mobile app development:** Enabling mobile apps to interact with backend services.

Examples of popular web APIs:

- **Twitter API:** Allows developers to access and manipulate Twitter data.

- **Google Maps API:** Provides mapping and geolocation services.

- **Facebook Graph API:** Enables developers to interact with Facebook data and features.

What is REST?

REST (Representational State Transfer) is an architectural style for designing distributed systems, particularly web services. It emphasizes simplicity, scalability, and statelessness.

Key principles of REST:

- **Statelessness:** Each request is treated independently, without relying on previous requests.

- **Client-Server Architecture:** The client-server model separates concerns between the client and server.

- **Cacheable:** Responses can be cached to improve performance.

- **Layered System:** The system can be layered to improve modularity and scalability.

- **Uniform Interface:** The API uses a uniform interface based on HTTP methods (GET, POST, PUT, DELETE) and resources.

RESTful APIs:

- **Use HTTP methods:** RESTful APIs use HTTP methods (GET, POST, PUT, DELETE) to represent actions on resources. For example, GET is used to retrieve data, POST to create data, PUT to update data, and DELETE to delete data.

- **Focus on resources:** RESTful APIs are centered around resources, which represent entities in the system (e.g., customers, products, orders).

- **Use URIs:** Resources are identified using URIs (Uniform Resource Identifiers).

- **Self-descriptive messages:** Responses include enough information for the client to understand the response and potentially take further action.

- **Statelessness:** Each request is treated independently, without relying on previous requests.

Benefits of REST:

- **Simplicity:** RESTful APIs are generally simpler to understand and implement compared to other architectural styles.

- **Scalability:** RESTful APIs are designed to be scalable, allowing them to handle large numbers of requests.

- **Flexibility:** RESTful APIs can be easily adapted to changing requirements.

- **Interoperability:** RESTful APIs can be easily integrated with different systems and platforms.

By following the REST principles, you can design and build efficient, scalable, and easy-to-use web APIs.

How do RESTful APIs differ from traditional web services?

RESTful APIs and **traditional web services** (often based on SOAP) have distinct characteristics, each with its own advantages and use cases.

Key Differences:

RESTful APIs

- **Focus on Resources:** Represent data as resources (e.g., customers, products) and use HTTP methods (GET, POST, PUT, DELETE) to interact with them.

- **Statelessness:** Each request is treated independently, without relying on previous requests.

- **Cacheability:** Responses can be cached to improve performance.

- **Layered System:** The system can be layered to improve modularity and scalability.

- **Uniform Interface:** Uses a uniform interface based on HTTP methods and URIs.

Traditional Web Services (SOAP)

- **Message-based:** Relies on XML-based messages and SOAP envelopes.

- **Stateful:** Can maintain state between requests.

- **Complex:** Requires more configuration and setup.

- **Security:** Often provides built-in security features like WS-Security.

Choosing Between RESTful APIs and Traditional Web Services:

- **Simplicity:** RESTful APIs are generally simpler to understand and implement.

- **Performance:** RESTful APIs can be more performant due to their lightweight nature.

- **Interoperability:** Both RESTful APIs and traditional web services can be interoperable, but RESTful APIs often have better cross-platform compatibility.

- **Specific Requirements:** Consider your specific requirements, such as the need for complex security features or the integration with existing systems.

History of ASP.NET Web API.

ASP.NET Web API emerged as a response to the growing need for building modern, efficient, and interoperable web APIs in the .NET ecosystem. Here's a timeline of its development:

Early 2000s: ASP.NET (Active Server Pages Network Enabled Technologies): Released as Microsoft's framework for developing web applications. It focused on building web pages with server-side scripting and user interaction.

2007-2008: Windows Communication Foundation (WCF): Introduced as a broader framework for building various types of services, including web services. However, WCF's complexity made it less ideal for simpler RESTful APIs.

2010: Emergence of RESTful APIs: REST (Representational State Transfer) gained significant traction as an architectural style for web services due to its simplicity, scalability, and platform independence.

2011: ASP.NET MVC 3: Released with a limited preview of "Web API" features. This initial iteration provided basic functionalities like routing, content negotiation, and model binding.

2012: ASP.NET Web API 1.0: Officially released as a standalone framework within the .NET ecosystem. It offered significant improvements over the limited preview, including:

- Enhanced routing capabilities

- Support for various HTTP verbs (GET, POST, PUT,

DELETE)

- Model binding and validation

- Content negotiation for returning data in different formats (JSON, XML)

- Built-in support for filtering and sorting data

<u>2014</u>: **ASP.NET Web API 2.0:** Introduced key features:

- Support for OData (Open Data Protocol) for querying data in a standardized way

- Attribute routing for cleaner and more organized code

- Integration with ASP.NET Identity for user authentication and authorization

<u>2016</u>: **ASP.NET Core 1.0:** Introduced ASP.NET Core as a complete rewrite of the .NET framework, designed to be modular, cross-platform, and open-source. However, ASP.NET Web API remained as a separate framework integrated with ASP.NET Core.

<u>2017 and Beyond</u>: **ASP.NET Core Web API:** With the release of ASP.NET Core 2.0, ASP.NET Web API became fully integrated into ASP.NET Core. This merged the strengths of both frameworks, offering:

- Modern and modular architecture

- Cross-platform support (Windows, Linux, macOS)

- Improved performance

- Seamless integration with other ASP.NET Core components like middleware

Current Status:

Today, ASP.NET Core Web API continues to evolve as part of the ASP.NET Core framework. It remains a popular choice for building

RESTful web APIs in the .NET ecosystem due to its ease of use, flexibility, and extensive community support.

Additional Notes:

- While ASP.NET Web API 1.x and 2.x are still supported for legacy applications, ASP.NET Core Web API is the recommended approach for new projects due to its modern architecture and cross-platform capabilities.

- There are ongoing efforts to improve ASP.NET Core Web API further, such as integrating with the new Minimal APIs feature in ASP.NET Core 6 and beyond.

How to design and develop RESTful APIs?

RESTful APIs are a popular approach for building web services that follow the Representational State Transfer (REST) architectural style. Here are some key principles and guidelines for designing and developing effective RESTful APIs:

1. Use HTTP Methods:

- **GET:** Retrieve data.

- **POST:** Create data.

- **PUT:** Update data.

- **DELETE:** Delete data.

- **PATCH:** Partially update data.

- **HEAD:** Retrieve metadata about a resource without the full response body.

- **OPTIONS:** Get information about the supported HTTP methods for a resource.

2. Identify Resources:

- Define the resources that your API will expose.

- Use nouns to name resources (e.g., "products", "users").

3. Use URIs to Represent Resources:

- Use URIs to identify resources uniquely.

- Follow a consistent URI structure.

4. Return Appropriate HTTP Status Codes:

- Use HTTP status codes to indicate the success or failure of a request.

- Common status codes include:

    - 200 OK

    - 201 Created

    - 400 Bad Request

    - 401 Unauthorized

    - 404 Not Found

    - 500 Internal Server Error

5. Use JSON or XML for Data Representation:

- Choose a suitable data format for your API.

- JSON is often preferred due to its simplicity and lightweight nature.

6. Implement Versioning:

- Consider versioning your API to support backward compatibility.

- Use URL versioning or header-based versioning.

7. Handle Errors Gracefully:

- Provide informative error messages and appropriate HTTP

status codes.

- Use validation to prevent invalid requests.

8. Consider Security:

- Implement authentication and authorization mechanisms to protect your API.

- Use HTTPS to encrypt data in transit.

9. Document Your API: Provide clear and concise documentation for your API, including:

- Resource definitions

- Supported HTTP methods

- Request and response formats

- Error codes

- Usage examples

Explain authentication in REST API.

Authentication is a crucial aspect of securing RESTful APIs. It ensures that only authorized users can access and interact with your API's resources. Here are some common authentication methods:

1. API Key Authentication:

- **Simple:** Assign a unique API key to each client or user.

- **Insecure:** API keys can be easily compromised if not handled securely.

- **Suitable for:** Public APIs with less sensitive data.

2. OAuth 2.0:

- **Standard:** A widely used authorization framework for web applications.

- **Security:** Provides robust security features like authorization codes, access tokens, and refresh tokens.

- **Suitable for:** Most modern applications, especially those that need to integrate with third-party services.

3. Basic Authentication:

- **Simple:** Requires a username and password.

- **Insecure:** Transmits credentials in plain text over the network.

- **Suitable for:** Internal APIs or APIs with low-security requirements.

4. JWT (JSON Web Token):

- **Token-based:** Issues a token to the client upon successful authentication.

- **Security:** Provides a secure and stateless way to authenticate users.

- **Suitable for:** APIs that need to issue tokens for access and authorization.

5. OpenID Connect:

- **Built on OAuth 2.0:** Extends OAuth 2.0 with features like identity federation and single sign-on.

- **Security:** Provides a high level of security and interoperability.

- **Suitable for:** APIs that need to integrate with other identity providers or enable single sign-on.

What are common API design patterns and best practices?

When designing RESTful APIs, it's essential to adhere to certain patterns and best practices to ensure they are easy to use, understand, and maintain. Here are some key principles:

Resource-Based Design

- **Identify Resources:** Clearly define the resources that your API exposes (e.g., products, users, orders).

- **Use Nouns for Resources:** Use nouns in URIs to represent resources (e.g., /products, /users).

- **Use HTTP Verbs:** Employ appropriate HTTP methods to represent actions on resources:

    - **GET:** Retrieve data

    - **POST:** Create data

    - **PUT:** Update data

    - **PATCH:** Partially update data

    - **DELETE:** Delete data

Consistent Naming and Structure

- Use consistent naming conventions for URIs, parameters, and headers.

- Maintain a clear and predictable structure for your API.

Error Handling

- Return informative error messages with appropriate HTTP status codes (e.g., 400 Bad Request, 401 Unauthorized, 500 Internal Server Error).

- Provide clear error messages to help developers understand and troubleshoot issues.

Versioning

- Implement versioning to support backward compatibility.

- Use URL versioning (e.g., /api/v1/products) or header-based versioning.

Pagination

- For large datasets, implement pagination to avoid overwhelming clients with excessive data.

- Use query parameters like page and pageSize to control pagination.

Filtering and Sorting

- Allow clients to filter and sort data using query parameters.

- Consider using OData for more complex filtering and sorting options.

Caching

- Implement caching to improve performance and reduce load on your backend.

- Use HTTP headers like Cache-Control to control caching behavior.

Security

- Implement authentication and authorization mechanisms to protect your API.

- Use HTTPS to encrypt data in transit.

- Consider using rate limiting to prevent abuse.

Documentation

- Provide clear and comprehensive documentation for your API, including:

  - Resource definitions

  - Supported HTTP methods

  - Request and response formats

  - Error codes

  - Usage examples

Additional Tips

- **Keep it Simple:** Avoid overcomplicating your API design.

- **Prioritize Readability:** Write clean and well-structured code that is easy to understand and maintain.

- **Test Thoroughly:** Test your API thoroughly to ensure it works as expected under various conditions.

- **Iterate and Improve:** Continuously evaluate and improve your API based on feedback and changing requirements.

How do I get and add a JWT token via Rest API?

Below are the comprehensive steps on how to get and add JWT tokens in REST APIs using C#:

Getting JWT Tokens:

1. **Generate Token:** Use a suitable library like Microsoft.Identi tyModel.Tokens or JWT.NET to generate the token. Provide the necessary claims (e.g., username, expiration time) and a secret key.

2. **Store Token:**

   - Store the generated token securely in a suitable location (e.g., local storage, session, database).

- ○ Consider using HttpOnly cookies for added security.

Adding JWT Tokens to REST API Requests:

1. **Authorization Header:** Include the token in the Authorization header of your HTTP requests. Use the Bearer scheme: Authorization: Bearer <token>.

```
using System.Net.Http;

using System.Net.Http.Headers;

public class ApiCaller

{

public async Task<string> CallProtectedApi(string token)

{

using (var httpClient = new HttpClient())

{

httpClient.DefaultRequestHeaders.Authorization = new AuthenticationHeaderValue("Bearer", token);

var response = await  httpClient.GetAsync("https://your-api-endpoint");

return await response.Content.ReadAsStringAsync();

}

}

}
```

1. **Query Parameter or Body:** Include the token as a query parameter or in the request body.

```
using System.Net.Http;

public class ApiCaller
```

```
{

public async Task<string> CallProtectedApi(string token)

{

using (var httpClient = new HttpClient())

{

var response = await httpClient.GetAsync($"https://your-api-endpoin
t?token={token}");

return await response.Content.ReadAsStringAsync();

}

}

}
```

Server-Side Validation:

1. **Extract Token:** Extract the token from the Authorization header, query parameter, or request body.

2. **Validate Token:** Use the same secret key and algorithm used to generate the token.

   ○ Verify the token's signature, expiration, and other claims.

```
using System.IdentityModel.Tokens.Jwt;

using System.Text;

using Microsoft.AspNetCore.Authorization;

using Microsoft.AspNetCore.Mvc;

[Authorize]

public class ValuesController : ControllerBase

{
```

```csharp
public IActionResult Get()

{

var token = Request.Headers["Authorization"].ToString().Replace("B
earer ", "");

var tokenHandler = new JwtSecurityTokenHandler();

var validationParameters = new TokenValidationParameters

{

ValidateIssuer = false,

ValidateAudience = false,

ValidateLifetime = true,

ValidateIssuerSigningKey = true,

IssuerSigningKey = new SymmetricSecurityKey(Encoding.UTF8.Get
Bytes("your-secret-key"))

};

try

{

tokenHandler.ValidateToken(token, validationParameters, out Securi-
tyToken validatedToken);

return Ok("Authorized");

}

catch (Exception ex)

{

return Unauthorized(ex.Message);

}
```

```
    }

}
```

What is the Difference Between PUT, POST, and PATCH in RESTful API?

In RESTful APIs, **HTTP methods** are used to communicate with web servers. Three common methods are PUT, POST, and PATCH. Each has a specific purpose:

PUT

- **Purpose:** Used to **update** an entire resource.

- **Behavior:** Replaces the existing resource with the new data provided in the request body.

- **Idempotency:** Performing a PUT request multiple times will always produce the same result.

POST

- **Purpose:** Used to **create** a new resource.

- **Behavior:** Sends data to the server, which creates a new resource. The server will typically return the newly created resource's identifier.

- **Non-idempotent:** Performing a POST request multiple times may create multiple resources.

PATCH

- **Purpose:** Used to **partially update** a resource.

- **Behavior:** Applies specific modifications to the existing resource based on the data provided in the request body.

- **Non-idempotent:** Performing a PATCH request multiple times may produce different results, depending on the specific modifications applied.

Key Differences:

Example:

Imagine you have a user resource with properties like id, name, and email.

- **PUT:** To update the entire user, you would send a PUT request to /users/123 with a request body containing the new values for name and email.

- **POST:** To create a new user, you would send a POST request to /users with a request body containing the initial values for name and email.

- **PATCH:** To update only the name property of a user, you would send a PATCH request to /users/123 with a request body containing the new name value.

How to address Idempotency in REST API using C#?

Idempotency is a fundamental principle in RESTful APIs, ensuring that multiple requests to the same resource produce the same result. Here are several strategies to address idempotency in your API:

1. HTTP Methods:

- **PUT:** By design, PUT requests are idempotent. They replace the entire resource, always resulting in the same state regardless of how many times they are executed.

- **PATCH:** While not inherently idempotent, PATCH requests can be made idempotent by carefully crafting the update operations. Avoid using conditional logic or side effects within the PATCH operation.

2. ETags (Entity Tags):

- **Conditional Requests:** Use ETags to implement conditional requests. An ETag is a unique identifier for a resource.

- **If-Match Header:** Send an If-Match header with the ETag of the resource you want to update. If the ETag matches the server's current ETag, the update is performed; otherwise, it's rejected.

- **If-None-Match Header:** Use If-None-Match to check if a resource has been modified since the last time it was fetched. If it hasn't, the server can return a 304 Not Modified response.

3. Idempotent Keys:

- **Unique Identifiers:** Ensure that each resource has a unique identifier (e.g., UUID).

- **Key-Based Operations:** Use this key to identify the resource and perform operations based on it. For example, a PUT request with a specific key will always update the corresponding resource.

4. Server-Side Idempotency Checks:

- **Unique Constraints:** Implement unique constraints on database columns to prevent duplicate entries.

- **Idempotent Logic:** If necessary, implement server-side logic to ensure idempotency, such as checking for existing records or performing conditional updates.

5. Token-Based Approaches:

- **Unique Tokens:** Generate unique tokens for each request.

- **Token Validation:** Validate the token on the server to ensure it's unique and hasn't been used before.

- **Token-Based Idempotency:** Use the token to identify a specific request and prevent duplicates.

Example:

PUT /users/123

Content-Type: application/json

```
If-Match: "etag-value"

{

"name": "John Doe"

}
```

In this example, the If-Match header ensures that the update is only performed if the current ETag matches the one provided in the request. This helps prevent conflicts and ensures idempotency.

```
using System.Net;

using System.Net.Http;

using System.Web.Http;

namespace YourNamespace.Controllers

{

public class UsersController : ApiController

{

// ... other controller methods

[HttpPut]

public HttpResponseMessage PutUser(int id, User user)

{

// Retrieve the existing user from your data source

var existingUser = GetUserById(id);

// Generate an ETag for the existing user

var etag = GenerateETag(existingUser);

// Check if the provided ETag matches the existing ETag
```

```csharp
var requestEtag = Request.Headers.IfMatch.FirstOrDefault()?.Entity
Tag;

if (requestEtag != null && requestEtag.StrongTag != etag)

{

return Request.CreateResponse(HttpStatusCode.PreconditionFailed
);

}

// Update the user with the new data

existingUser.Name = user.Name;

// ... other updates

// Save the updated user to your data source

// Return a response with the updated ETag

return Request.CreateResponse(HttpStatusCode.OK, existingUser,
CreateEntityTag(existingUser));

}

// ... other controller methods

private string GenerateETag(User user)

{

// Implement your ETag generation logic here

// For example, you could use a hash of the user's ID and properties

return $"{user.Id}-{CalculateHash(user)}";

}

private EntityTagHeaderValue CreateEntityTag(User user)

{
```

```
return   new   EntityTagHeaderValue(new   EntityTag(GenerateE-
Tag(user), true));

    }

  }

}
```

Explanation:

1. **Generate ETag:** For each user, generate a unique ETag based on the user's properties.

2. **Check If-Match Header:** In the PUT method, check if the request includes an If-Match header with a matching ETag.

3. **Conditional Update:** If the ETags match, proceed with the update. If not, return a PreconditionFailed response.

4. **Return Updated ETag:** In the response, include the updated ETag to allow clients to use it for subsequent requests.

Additional Considerations:

- **ETag Generation:** Choose an appropriate ETag generation algorithm that ensures uniqueness and reflects changes to the resource.

- **Strong vs. Weak ETags:** Consider using strong ETags for precise matching and weak ETags for caching purposes.

- **Error Handling:** Implement proper error handling to catch exceptions and return appropriate HTTP status codes.

- **Idempotency for Other Operations:** Apply similar techniques for other operations like PATCH to ensure idempotency.

What are Strong and Weak ETags in Rest API and how they're implemented?

Below is the comprehensive explanation of strong and weak ETags in RESTful APIs and their implementation in C#:

Strong ETags:

- **Purpose:** Provide a precise match for resource updates.

- **Behavior:** If the ETag in the request matches the server's ETag, the update is allowed. Otherwise, it's rejected.

- **Use Cases:** Ideal for scenarios where exact matching of resource content is crucial, such as preventing data corruption or overwriting changes made by other clients.

Weak ETags:

- **Purpose:** Used for caching purposes.

- **Behavior:** If the ETag in the request matches the server's ETag, the server can return a 304 Not Modified response, indicating that the resource hasn't changed.

- **Use Cases:** Suitable for resources that are frequently accessed but rarely modified, as it can reduce network traffic and server load.

Implementation in C#:

1. Generating ETags:

```csharp
private string GenerateStrongETag(Resource resource)

{

// Calculate a hash based on the resource's content

var hash = CalculateHash(resource);

return $"W/{hash}"; // Weak ETag
```

```
}

private string GenerateWeakETag(Resource resource)

{

// Calculate a hash based on the resource's metadata (e.g., last modified
time)

var hash = CalculateHash(resource.LastModified);

return $"W/{hash}"; // Weak ETag

}
```

2. Using ETags in Requests and Responses:

```
[HttpPut]

public HttpResponseMessage PutResource(int id, Resource resource)

{

// Retrieve the existing resource

var existingResource = GetResourceById(id);

// Generate a strong ETag for the existing resource

var strongETag = GenerateStrongETag(existingResource);

// Check if the request includes an If-Match header with a matching
ETag

var requestEtag = Request.Headers.IfMatch.FirstOrDefault()?.Entity
Tag;

if (requestEtag != null && requestEtag.StrongTag != strongETag)

{

return Request.CreateResponse(HttpStatusCode.PreconditionFailed
);

}
```

```csharp
// Update the resource

UpdateResource(existingResource, resource);

// Return a response with the updated ETag

return Request.CreateResponse(HttpStatusCode.OK, existingResource, CreateEntityTag(existingResource));

}

[HttpGet]

public HttpResponseMessage GetResource(int id)

{

var resource = GetResourceById(id);

var weakETag = GenerateWeakETag(resource);

// Add the weak ETag to the response headers

var response = Request.CreateResponse(HttpStatusCode.OK, resource);

response.Headers.ETag = new EntityTagHeaderValue(new EntityTag(weakETag));

return response;

}
```

Key Points:

- **Strong ETags:** Use for precise matching and to prevent data corruption.

- **Weak ETags:** Use for caching and to reduce network traffic.

- **ETag Generation:** Choose an appropriate hashing algorithm based on your requirements.

- **Conditional Requests:** Use If-Match and If-None-Match headers to leverage ETags for conditional requests.

- **Response Headers:** Include the ETag in the response headers for subsequent requests.

Explain CRUD mapping to HTTP Verbs in REST API.

In RESTful APIs, the HTTP verbs (methods) are used to represent different operations on resources. The most common mapping is known as CRUD (Create, Read, Update, Delete).

CRUD Mapping to HTTP Verbs:

Example:

```
using System.Net;

using System.Net.Http;

using System.Web.Http;

namespace YourNamespace.Controllers

{

public class ProductsController : ApiController

{

// ... other controller methods

[HttpGet]

public IEnumerable<Product> GetProducts()

{

// Retrieve all products from your data source

return products;

}

[HttpGet]
```

```csharp
public Product GetProduct(int id)

{

// Retrieve a specific product by ID

return products.FirstOrDefault(p => p.Id == id);

}

[HttpPost]

public HttpResponseMessage PostProduct(Product product)

{

// Create a new product

products.Add(product);

return Request.CreateResponse(HttpStatusCode.Created, product);

}

[HttpPut]

public void PutProduct(int id, Product product)

{

// Update an existing product

var existingProduct = products.FirstOrDefault(p => p.Id == id);

if (existingProduct != null)

{

existingProduct.Name = product.Name;  // ... update other properties

}

}

[HttpDelete]
```

```csharp
public void DeleteProduct(int id)

{

// Delete a product

var productToDelete = products.FirstOrDefault(p => p.Id == id);

if (productToDelete != null)

{

products.Remove(productToDelete);

}

}

}

}
```

Explanation:

- **GET:** Used to retrieve resources (e.g., GetProducts, GetProduct).

- **POST:** Used to create new resources (e.g., PostProduct).

- **PUT:** Used to update an entire resource (e.g., PutProduct).

- **DELETE:** Used to delete a resource (e.g., DeleteProduct).

 Note:

- **PUT vs. PATCH:** While both are used for updates, PUT replaces the entire resource, while PATCH updates specific properties.

- **HTTP Status Codes:** The controller methods typically return appropriate HTTP status codes (e.g., 200 OK, 201 Created, 404 Not Found) to indicate the result of the operation.

- **Data Validation:** Implement proper data validation to ensure that incoming data is valid before performing operations.

- **Error Handling:** Handle potential errors and return informative error responses.

What are the various ways to manage errors in .NET Core for web APIs?

Effective error handling is crucial for building robust and user-friendly web APIs. In .NET Core, there are several strategies you can employ to manage errors gracefully:

1. Exception Filters

- **Purpose:** Intercept and handle exceptions that occur during the request pipeline.

- **How to use:**

  - Create a class that implements the IExceptionFilter interface.

  - Override the OnException method to handle the exception.

  - Register the exception filter in your Startup.cs file.

2. Middleware

- **Purpose:** Custom middleware can be used to handle specific errors or implement custom error handling logic.

- **How to use:**

  - Create a middleware class that implements the IMiddleware interface.

  - Handle exceptions within the Invoke method.

  - Add the middleware to your request pipeline in Startup.cs.

3. Global Error Handling

- **Purpose:** Centralize error handling for the entire application.

- **How to use:** Implement the IExceptionHandler interface in a global error handler. Register the handler in your Startup.cs file.

4. Custom Error Pages

- **Purpose:** Provide informative and user-friendly error messages.

- **How to use:** Create custom error pages and configure them in your Startup.cs file using the UseStatusCodePages middleware.

5. Logging

- **Purpose:** Record errors for debugging and analysis.

- **How to use:** Use the built-in logging framework in .NET Core to log exceptions and other relevant information. Configure logging levels and providers in your appsettings.json file.

6. HTTP Status Codes

- **Purpose:** Return appropriate HTTP status codes to indicate the nature of errors.

- **How to use:** Return specific HTTP status codes (e.g., 400, 401, 404, 500) based on the type of error.

7. Problem Details

- **Purpose:** Return structured error responses that can be easily consumed by clients.

- **How to use:** Use the ProblemDetails class to create detailed error responses with information like the error message, status code, and additional context.

8. Custom Error Responses

- **Purpose:** Return custom error responses tailored to your specific needs.

- **How to use:** Create custom error response models and return them from your API controllers.

Example using Exception Filters:

public class MyExceptionFilter : IExceptionFilter

{

public void OnException(ExceptionContext context)

{

if (context.Exception is

ArgumentNullException)

{

// Handle ArgumentNullException

context.Result = new BadRequestObjectResult("Argument is null.");

}

else

{

// Handle other exceptions

context.Result = new StatusCodeResult(500);

}

}

}

—·—

LAND YOUR DREAM .NET JOB:
DON'T WING YOUR INTERVIEW!

A re you a talented developer ready to take the next step in your career? .NET positions are booming, but competition is fierce. Don't gamble your future on outdated resources or winging the interview.

The "Mastering the .NET Core Interview" Book is your one-stop shop for success. It's not just another question bank. This comprehensive guide dives deep into the essential knowledge you need to impress any interviewer.

Imagine confidently discussing:

☐☐Interview Questions and Concepts related to MVC

☐☐Utilizing Asynchronous Programming in C# to create robust applications.

☐☐Understand Web API and REST API with grace and clarity.

☐☐Understand .NET Core concepts efficiently.

☐☐Understand the fundamentals of ASP.NET Core.

The "Mastering the .NET Core Interview" Book equips you with the knowledge, confidence, and interview strategies to land your dream .NET job. Don't settle for anything less. Get your copy today!

—◈◈◈—

MAY I ASK YOU FOR A SMALL FAVOR?

I want to express my sincere gratitude for choosing to invest your time in reading this book. Your decision to explore this work among countless others means a lot to me.

I hope that within these pages, you've discovered actionable insights that can enhance your daily life. Your journey doesn't have to end here, though.

May I kindly request an additional 30 seconds of your valuable time?

Sharing your thoughts about the book through a review would be immensely appreciated. Your review serves as a beacon, guiding other readers to take a chance on my books. It's a small gesture that carries significant weight in the world of authors.

To submit your review effortlessly, please click on the link below. It will take you directly to the book's review page:

"Mastering the .NET Core Interview"

Alternatively, you can also find the "**Reviews Section**" of this book's page on Amazon.

Your review will require just a minute of your time but will make a monumental difference in helping me connect with a broader audience and I eagerly look forward to reading your review.

Once again, thank you for your unwavering support of my work.

DISCLAIMER

This book is for educational purposes only. Readers acknowledge that the author does not render legal, financial, medical, or professional advice. The content within this book has been derived from various sources. Please consult a licensed professional before attempting any techniques outlined in this book.

By reading this document, the reader agrees that under no circumstances is the author responsible for any direct or indirect losses incurred as a result of the use of the information contained within this document, including but not limited to errors, omissions, or inaccuracies.

Adherence to all applicable laws and regulations, including international, federal, state, and local governing professional licensing, business practices, advertising, and all other jurisdictions, is the sole responsibility of the purchaser or reader.

Neither the author nor the publisher assumes any responsibility or liability whatsoever on behalf of the purchaser or reader of these materials. Any perceived slight of any individual or organization is purely unintentional.